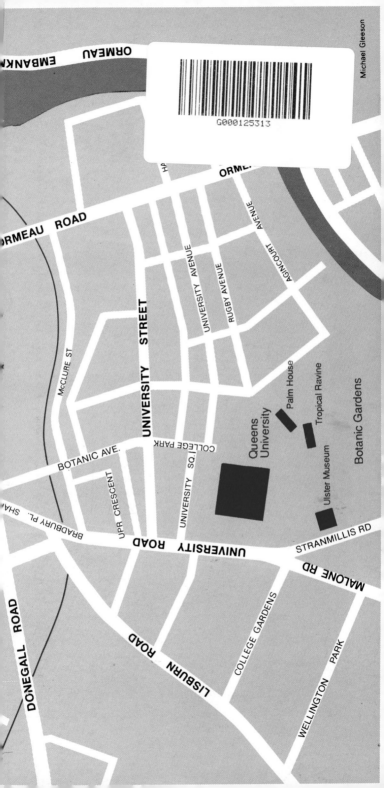

MARY DOWEY

THE BEST OF
BELFAST

A & A FARMAR

© Mary Dowey 1995

British Library Cataloguing in Publication Data
A CIP catalogue record for this book
is available from the British Library

Text and cover design by Rai Uhlemann
Index by Helen Litton
Typesetting by A. & A. Farmar
Maps by Michael Gleeson
Ordnance Survey Permit No 818
Printed by Betaprint
Photographs: cover, title page, pp 6–7, 18, 22, 23,
26–7, 30, 38, 43, 46, 51 (top), 74, 79, 90, 94 by
Chris Hill; pp 15, 35, 39, 42, 47, 51, 54, 55, 58, 59,
62, 63, 67, 70, 71, 91 by Rai Uhlemann; 11, 66, 83
from the Lawrence Collection

ISBN 1 899047 07 7

ACKNOWLEDGEMENTS

Without the support, encouragement and inside
information provided by a large number of
people, this book would have been a very puny
effort. In particular I would like to thank
Margaret O'Reilly and Jackie D'Arcy of the
Northern Ireland Tourist Board, Gerry Lennon
of Belfast City Council and the following
informants and helpers:
Hugo Boylan, Clare Connery, Dorothy and Liz
Dowey, John Gray, Chris Hill, Neil Maclaren,
Anne and Sarah-Jane McMullan, Harry
Morrison, Eamonn Ó Catháin, Sean Rafferty,
Barbara Anne Slevin, Mahen and Sumanthra
Varma, Jenny Watson.

Published by A. & A. Farmar
Beech House
78 Ranelagh Village
Dublin 6
Ireland

CONTENTS

INTRODUCTION

The grand old Victorian buildings are being restored. The new Lagan Weir has put wildlife back into a stretch of river poisoned, until recently, by pollution. As ugly 1960s office blocks come down, so that you now glimpse hills at the end of streets, Belfast is looking up—feeling upbeat. The pubs and restaurants are crammed, until one or two o'clock in the morning, with people out enjoying themselves. After a quarter of a century languishing in notoriety, this is suddenly the place to be.

When I was a child growing up in Belfast, the things I liked most about the city had nothing much to do with its physical substance. I don't believe I ever really looked at the fine brick warehouses on Bedford Street, or the slender pinnacle of the Albert Memorial—Belfast's miniature Big Ben, listing slightly to one side—nor even the haughty grey-white mass of the City Hall.

My Belfast was a place of far more

Belfast by night

tangible pleasures. Sunday walks along the Lagan towpath; huge high teas with Ormeau bakery bread; occasional glimpses of my father on the miscroscopic stage of the first Lyric Theatre; excursions with my mother into the perfumed air of Robinson & Cleaver which I believed to be the most regal department store in the world . . . For a long time after I grew up and moved away, those were the things that lodged in the top layer of memory, above the shipyard cranes that stand like giant yellow goalposts against the sky.

Curled around the natural harbour of Belfast Lough and sheltered by a semi-circle of mountains, Belfast's setting is spectacular. That does not mean that the city itself is beautiful. Like other great Victorian cities across the Irish Sea — Glasgow, Manchester, Bradford, Leeds— Belfast was shaped by industry. Cotton, linen, shipbuilding, ropemaking, engineering, tobacco—those were the trades that enabled it to grow more rapidly, towards the end of the nineteenth century, than any other city in Europe. The birthplace of the *Titanic* was a Titan of commerce. It ploughed its prosperity into streets of houses for the workers, in rusty Belfast brick, and a multitude of grandiose public buildings enshrining civic pride.

It was not until the Troubles began to tear the heart out of the place that Belfast's finest features came to be appreciated—not just appreciated but salvaged, with typically gritty Belfast resolve. People here are not easily put off. 'See Belfast, devout and profane and hard,' wrote the poet Louis MacNeice—rather hard, himself, in his judgment of a place that has always kept its spirit, even in extraordinarily difficult times. Returning to Belfast regularly over the years, I have marvelled at the way people have kept smiling. 'Ah, sure life goes on,' they say. Plucky cheerfulness has kept businesses going, the theatres open, the Ulster Orchestra playing, even through the blackest times.

Belfast people are blunt, but they are also friendly and very funny. 'It is impossible to be gloomy for long in Belfast,' Dervla Murphy says in *A Place Apart*, the book which records her journey around the North towards the end of the 1970s, when sectarian divisions were deepening almost daily. 'I was feeling rather depressed one afternoon when I turned a corner and saw on a gable-end the familiar NO POPE HERE. And underneath, in a different coloured paint, LUCKY OLD POPE!'

That good humour is one of the things that makes Belfast such a marvellous place to visit. The buoyant atmosphere peace has brought is another. As far as I can determine, *The Best of Belfast* is the first independent visitors' guidebook to this revitalised, buzzing city of half a million people. Although I hope it contains all the essential information anybody might need to make the most of their stay, it is not intended to be comprehensive. Far from it. Instead, it's a deliberate attempt to pick out Belfast's very best features and describe them in a way that captures the flavour of the city. To some extent it is a personal book, written after months of on-the-spot research, and not everybody may agree with the final omissions and inclusions. But the main point this book makes should provoke no argument at all. Belfast has more good things to offer now than ever before.

A BRIEF HISTORY

A thousand years ago there was no town of Belfast at all—only a fording point across the Lagan at the mud flats which determined the name—*béal feirste* in Irish, the mouth of the sandspit. In the twelfth century its defences were strengthened with a castle, built by the Anglo-Norman knight adventurer John de Courcy in 1177. Gradually Norman power was eroded, however, in repeated onslaughts from the local Gaelic chieftains, the O'Neills of Clandeboye. It was not until the end of the sixteenth century, when the Tudor conquest of Ulster was well under way, that their supremacy was finally undermined.

In 1603 Sir Arthur Chichester was sent by James I to mastermind the Plantation of Ulster, bringing in his wake thousands of Lowland Scots who were to help keep the rebel Irish under control. That year, the fledgling Belfast was granted a charter of incorporation, giving it the status of a borough—the first step towards its future as a major city.

By 1660, the time of the Restoration, Belfast was a small but prosperous port, shipping beef, butter and corn from Plantation farms abroad, especially to France. As municipal power lay in the hands of the Protestant Ascendancy and

Scottish and English settlers continued to pour in, Belfast's population was overwhelmingly Protestant. In 1708, the sovereign (the equivalent of mayor) reported: 'We have not amongst us in the town above seven Papists'—and this at a time when Catholics accounted for three-quarters of the population of Ireland as a whole.

Soon, English determination to enforce the Penal Laws against Catholics and other non-Anglicans threw the town's middle-class Presbyterians and Catholics together in a potent alliance to wrest power and basic rights from the ruling class. The eighteenth century, the Age of Enlightenment, lived up to its name in Belfast—a fact largely obscured by more recent events. Inspired by the American War of Independence and French stirrings towards revolution, a group of merchants

Donegall Place and the Royal Hotel *c.* 1860

11

led by Henry Joy McCracken and the Dublin revolutionary Wolfe Tone founded the Society of United Irishmen in 1791. Dedicated to replacing the connection with England by 'a cordial union among all the people of Ireland', it was to founder in the failed 1798 Rebellion. McCracken and other leading rebels were hanged, several Presbyterian ministers among them. England then disbanded the Irish parliament, introducing direct rule from London with the Act of Union in 1801.

By the beginning of the nineteenth century, Belfast had begun to expand, nurtured by the burgeoning cotton industry. Prosperity brought improvements to the port and streets; gas lighting was installed in 1823 for the dazzling sum of £40,000—a manifestation of typical Belfast fervour to smarten the town up. But the spirit of liberalism which had earlier united citizens of different religions was extinguished. Protestants anxiously watched their influence dwindle and southern support for Daniel O'Connell's movement for Catholic Emancipation grow. Already in 1832 there had been the first sectarian riots— establishing a pattern of sporadic violence that was to continue indefinitely. By 1840, with the drift of largely Catholic rural labourers towards the mushrooming town, a third of Belfast's population was Catholic.

A cotton mill fire in 1828 had had enormous consequences for Belfast's economic future. The owners, Mulhollands, decided to rebuild it as a linen mill, using cotton industrial technology to replace a tedious hand operation with the power-spinning of wet flax. That innovation, quickly copied, turned Belfast into the linen capital of the world and the fastest growing city in the British Empire, its population shooting up from 70,000 in 1840 to 350,000—a five-fold increase—by the end of the century.

The linen boom was supported by strong engineering and shipbuilding industries, with Harland & Wolff destined, by the 1880s, to become the greatest shipyard in the world, providing ships for the most widespread empire yet seen. By the turn of the century, Belfast could also lay claim to the largest ropeworks, the biggest tea machinery works, the most sizeable tobacco factory anywhere. Grandiose civic and commercial buildings sprang up. 'Parlour houses' with a front room and neat front garden began to take the place of the more basic 'kitchen houses' built earlier for linen workers. Belfast's remarkable economic might was officially recognised in 1888 with the arrival of Queen Victoria granting city status.

Politically, however, the situation was much less stable. In the second half of the nineteenth century, sectarian unrest continued to polarise the community. With nationalism growing in Irish politics, the pressure for Home Rule from Britain intensified, fuelling Unionist fears of Catholic domination and consequent economic decline. Under the Empire, with its vast trading network, Belfast had blossomed. In an independent Ireland, it might not fare so well.

As the move towards Home Rule gathered momentum in the early years of the century, the Unionists rallied to oppose it—with force if necessary. Ironically it was the vigour of the Unionist response to the possibility of Home Rule that stimulated the physical force wing of the Nationalist movement to arm themselves. Only the outbreak of the First World War in 1914 deflected energy from looming internal conflict. In 1916 two events illustrated the growing divergence between the largely Catholic Nationalists and the largely Protestant Unionists. At Easter Pearse and his followers staged the Rising in Dublin and in July, in the battle of the Somme, 5,500 men from the Ulster Division were killed—an enormous sacrifice which cemented the common feeling between Britain and the Northern Unionists. Ulster could no longer be forced into an independent Ireland. Instead, Home Rule for north and south separately was proposed. In 1921, with Civil War brewing in the south, Northern Ireland came into being with Belfast as its capital.

The timing could hardly have been worse. The Depression, felt internationally in the late Twenties, began in 1919 in Belfast and lasted for the best part of 20 years, crippling major industries. Shipbuilding suffered after the sinking of the *Titanic* on her maiden voyage in 1912; linen was hit as the market for luxury goods contracted. In the economic gloom, the old sectarian hatreds flared again, this time with the involvement of the IRA who had carried their Civil War campaign north. There was a brief episode in the 1930s when Protestant and Catholic working class protested together against conditions—taking the music hall song 'Yes, we have no bananas' as their theme tune, since almost every other song they knew had party connotations. This rapport did not, alas, last.

The Second World War brought respite, with shipyard and aircraft production

A gable-end mural in a Loyalist area

stepped up, and the two communities united in grief when the 1941 Blitz left over 700 Belfast people dead and large areas of the city devastated. Soon the welfare state improved housing, health and in particular education, but underlying frictions persisted. Catholic areas in particular had pockets of high unemployment and poor housing. A long-established system of patronage, politically justified by (and in turn reinforcing) Catholic nationalist lack of enthusiasm for the state, kept Protestants in power in the corporation and in control of the majority of jobs.

When the new Civil Rights Association marched in Derry in 1968, demanding equal votes for all in council elections, there were violent scenes. In August 1969, much more serious violence engulfed Belfast, prompting Britain to send in her army. By 1970 the Provisional IRA had also moved in, launching a campaign aimed at British withdrawal. The rest is televised, media-saturated history. Belfast was to remain a war zone for the next 25 years.

BEST PLACES TO STAY

B elfast offers a wide choice of accommodation at every price level, with spick-and-span guest houses particularly impressive for that winning combination of comfort and value. Attention to detail is generally high: even in many of the less expensive places you will find that your room has television, tea and coffee tray, hairdrier etc, and a full Ulster breakfast is almost always included in the price.

In the places listed below there is a bias towards the south side of the city, simply for the convenience of most visitors: on the axis south from the City Hall to the university area and beyond there are more restaurants and entertainments of various kinds than in any other direction.

For a more extensive list, consult Belfast City Council's free brochure, *Belfast and Proud*. The Northern Ireland Tourist Board (St Anne's Court, 59 North St, tel 246 609) is helpful with advice and reservations; and if you should happen to find yourself bedless late at night, its 24-hour tourist information screen outside the office door may provide the answer. Better to plan ahead: many good hotels offer extremely tempting rates for short breaks, especially at weekends.

PRICE GUIDE
(based on rate per night for single room)
Expensive—over £75
Moderate—£50–75
Inexpensive—£30–50
Budget—under £30

EUROPA HOTEL
Gt Victoria St, tel 327 000, fax 327 800.
Belfast's biggest city-centre hotel has risen, Phoenix-like, from the wreckage of innumerable bombs and after a complete multi-million pound overhaul in 1994 looks grander than ever. The bedrooms in this four-star establishment—flagship of the wellknown Hastings Hotels group—aren't enormous but they are furnished to a high standard, and the hotel's restaurant, brasserie, nightclub, two bars and extensive conference facilities cater for most needs. 179 rooms. 5 suites. 24-hour room service.
Expensive, but major reductions at weekends.

DUKES HOTEL
65–67 University St, tel 236 666, fax 237 177.
The chrome and black leather chairs in the lobby set the tone for one of Belfast's most streamlined, modern hotels—a light, airy place created out of an old building. The stylish bar in Dukes is a popular haunt—this is the university district, after all—and the restaurant is small but smart. Bedrooms are surprisingly spacious (almost all are doubles) and there's a nice little gym with his and her's saunas. Conference facilities. 21 rooms. 24-hour room service.
Expensive, but major reductions at weekends.

STORMONT HOTEL
587 Upr Newtownards Rd, tel 658 621, fax 480 240. Four miles out from the city centre on the main route to Strangford Lough, the Stormont is a large, purpose-built modern hotel which offers high standards of comfort and service. A member of the Hastings Hotels group, it is particularly well equipped for business visitors. Conference facilities. 106 rooms. 2 suites. 8 self-catering apartments.
Expensive, but weekend rates are attractive and apartments good value.

WELLINGTON PARK HOTEL
21 Malone Rd, tel 381 111, fax 665 410. A landmark of the university area since the 1950s although now extended and facelifted out of recognition, the Wellington Park has remained consistently popular. Its appeal extends beyond accommodation to its bars (*see* Best Nightlife p 81), which overflow with local socialisers at

Europa
Hotel

Malone
Lodge

weekends. Some rooms with jacuzzi/steambath.
Conference facilities. 50 rooms. *Moderate/
expensive, with major weekend reductions.*

MALONE LODGE
60 Eglantine Ave, tel 382 409, fax 382 706. In
a leafy avenue of Victorian terrace houses a
mile-and-a-half out of town is this highly
regarded new hotel. The style is traditional
rather than stark modern, with flounces and
flowery prints. The bedrooms are among the
biggest and brightest you will find anywhere; the
diningroom is crisply appointed and there is a
clubby feel to the Chestnut Bar. Conference

facilities. 33 rooms. *Moderate, with substantial reductions at weekends.*

OAKHILL COUNTRY HOUSE
59 Dunmurry Lane, tel 610 658, fax 621 566.
A few years ago owner May Noble was asked to entertain 300 wine growers at a reception in her magnificent gardens. The word spread on the grapevine: now guests from all over the world come to sample the elegance and warmth of her country house just five miles from the city centre. Rose growers note, it is right beside Sir Thomas and Lady Dixon Park (*see* Best Places to Visit, p 31). 4 rooms, all furnished with antiques, all en suite. Tea/coffee on request. *Moderate.*

THE OLD RECTORY
148 Malone Rd, tel 667 882. Two miles out of town, in one of the Malone Road's fine Victorian houses, an energetic young couple have recently created a delightful and distinctive small guest house. The Old Rectory has an appropriate old-world air, with antique furniture and beautiful linen. Fresh flowers and open fires add to the charm. Evening meal on tray in room if requested. 4 rooms—2 en suite, 2 with private bathrooms, all with TV, tea/coffee facilities, hairdrier. *Moderate.*

ROSELEIGH HOUSE
19 Rosetta Pk, tel 644 414. Just off the Ormeau Road, less than two miles southeast of the centre, this Victorian house recently turned guest house is in a quiet suburban park. It's sunny and spotless, the rooms feel fresh and evening meals are provided if required. Tea/coffee on request. 7 rooms including 1 family room, all en suite with TV. *Inexpensive.*

MALONE GUEST HOUSE
79 Malone Rd, tel 669 565. Ms Elsie McClure's simple but well-run guest house, in a double-fronted Victorian villa just over a mile from the city centre, enjoys repeat business both from business people and tourists (some from Japan, where she is featured in a guide). 8 rooms, all en suite, with TV and tea/coffee facilities. *Inexpensive and with weekend reductions.*

WINDERMERE GUEST HOUSE
60 Wellington Pk, tel 662 693. Academics during the week, families at weekends and foreign tourists at any time at all make up the clientele of the Murray sisters. Their guest house, plain but welcoming, is at the Lisburn Road end of Wellington Park, near shops and inexpensive restaurants. 8 rooms—2 en suite, all with TV. Tea/coffee on request. *Budget.*

BELFAST INTERNATIONAL YOUTH HOSTEL
22–32 Donegall Rd, tel 315 435. Off Shaftesbury Sq—a hot spot for young people at night, mid-way between the city centre and the university. So popular, it's often booked out weekends in advance. It has everything a hostel should have: free hot showers on all floors, a restaurant open 7.30 am–8 pm, large TV lounge, secure car park and bicycle storage, 24-hour staffing, laundry service. 5 minutes' walk from bus station and Botanic train station. 120 beds, most in 2 and 4-bedded rooms. *Budget.*

OUT OF TOWN

CULLODEN HOTEL
Bangor Rd, Craigavad, Co. Down, tel 425 223. Originally the Palace of the Bishops of Down, the Culloden is a luxury hotel whose Scottish Baronial grandeur and fine situation overlooking Belfast Lough make it popular for conferences, weddings and other special occasions. 6 miles from city centre. Health spa, tennis, beauty salon. 84 bedrooms, 8 suites. 24-hour room service. *Expensive, but with weekend reductions.*

RAYANNE HOUSE
60 Demesne Rd, Holywood, Co Down, tel 425 859. Raymond and Anne McClelland ran the Schooner restaurant in Holywood before opening their elegant Victorian home to guests who still enjoy their cooking: they are recent winners of the Northern Ireland Galtee Breakfast Award and provide impressive evening meals. 4 miles from Belfast. 6 rooms including 1 family room, all en suite with TV, tea/coffee facilities. *Inexpensive with weekend reductions.*

BEST PLACES TO VISIT

Although you might not think it if you arrive by car and find yourself transported along complicated one-way loops, Belfast city centre is surprisingly compact. There are plenty of interesting places to visit within relatively easy reach of the City Hall, with Queen's University and the Botanic Gardens just a mile to the south. For Belfast Castle, Belfast Zoo, Stormont or some of the parks on the outskirts, however, you will need to take your car or try out Belfast's efficient bus system.

For a quick but comprehensive introduction to the city, you might consider a Citybus sightseeing trip. The *Belfast: A Living History* tour incorporates all the most interesting facets of the city in a two-and-a-half hour circuit which takes in the Falls, the Shankill and other flashpoints of recent history as well as intriguing relics of the more distant past. Be sure to obtain the unusually handsome tour brochure. Tours run three days a week in summer, one day a week in winter. *For information and advance booking, tel 458 484.*

CITY HALL
Donegall Sq. Better than any street signs or any compass, the great green dome of the City Hall, visible for miles, gives Belfast visitors their bearings. When Queen Victoria conferred city status on a town of extraordinary industrial might in 1888, the need was felt to respond with a civic building of appropriate magnificence. Almost twenty years later, the City Hall—modelled on St Paul's Cathedral in London—was completed by the architect Brumwell Thomas, who was granted a knighthood for his efforts but had to sue to extract his fees. This vast, neo-classical palace in Portland stone is even more impressive inside than out, with its

grand marble staircase, whispering gallery and sumptuous plasterwork decorating the elaborately panelled dome. Look out for the mural on the landing by the Belfast artist John Luke, depicting the industries which made the city prosperous enough to afford architectural extravagance to this degree. *Free guided tours daily July–Sept 2.30 pm, Oct–June Weds only 10.30 am. Check with Belfast City Council, tel 320 202.*

City Hall

CROWN LIQUOR SALOON
44 Gt Victoria St. With fake Victorian bars springing up everywhere from Newtownards to New York, Belfast can gloat that it has taken good care of a genuine article of unparalleled magnificence. The Crown was built in 1885 by Patrick Flanagan, a student of architecture from Banbridge who brought back flamboyant ideas from his travels in Spain and Italy. His gorgeous gin palace is an intoxicating mixture of richly coloured tiles, stained glass, old gas lights and carved oak-panelled snugs like railway compartments. Even the gunmetal plates on

Crown
Liquor
Saloon

which Victorians struck their matches are still in place on the walls. This 'many-coloured cavern', as the poet John Betjeman glowingly described it, is in the care of the National Trust but still functions merrily as one of Belfast's best loved bars. (*See* Best Bars, p 44).

GRAND OPERA HOUSE
Gt Victoria St. Across the road from the Crown, the Grand Opera House is another architectural extravaganza, bravely and carefully restored time and again, like the old liquor saloon, after a series of bombs. It was designed in 1894 by the well known theatre architect Frank Matcham, inspired by fin-de-siècle fascination with the East. The fanciful turrets and curlicues outside are positively sober compared to the opulence within. The

gilded balconies and proscenium arch are lavishly decorated with exotic eastern motifs, and above it all is the marvellous ceiling painted by the Belfast artist Cherith McKinstry as part of the 1970s restoration. It's almost worth booking a show for the sumptuousness of the setting. (*See* Best Entertainment, p 74).

Grand
Opera
House

23

LINEN HALL LIBRARY

17 Donegall Sq North. Belfast's oldest library, founded in 1788 in the old White Linen Hall and later comfortably housed in this Charles Lanyon building, may not be an essential stopping point on a typical Belfast sightseeing tour—but for anybody genuinely interested in the city's past, it is a treat. The library has an exceptional collection of books relating to Irish and local history, some of them extremely old and rare, and is also famous for its 'Political Collection' of over 80,000 documents on every aspect of political life in Northern Ireland since 1968. Radicalism and liberalism are in the fabric of the Linen Hall: an early librarian was the United Irishman, Thomas Russell, hanged in 1803 for his support of Robert Emmet's uprising in Dublin. A free day pass is cheerfully offered to any visitor who wants to browse, and a café encourages lingering in a delightful Edwardian ambiance. *Open Mon–Fri 9.30 am–5.30 pm except Thurs late opening until 8.30pm, Sat 9.30 am–4 pm.*

ST MALACHY'S CHURCH

Alfred St. In a city of high Victoriana, here is something entirely different: a rare opportunity to see a splendid Tudor Revival church. With its octangular corner turrets and stone castellations, the exterior of St Malachy's, opened in 1842, looks more like a castle than a church. Inside, Henry VII's chapel at Westminster Abbey is the inspiration for an extraordinarily ornate fan-vaulted ceiling, which looks as if it had been piped on an upside-down cake, using the fanciest icing attachment. The carved white marble altar and canopied pulpit are equally elaborate but not original: both date from a 1926 restoration.

ST ANNE'S CATHEDRAL

Lr Donegall St. Opinions are divided on the aesthetic merits of Belfast's Anglican cathedral, which is actually much younger than it looks. Some admire its solid, unfussy neo-Romanesque grandeur; others find it coldly austere and strangely disappointing inside. Whichever way you view it, St Anne's is a Belfast landmark. Begun in 1899 and not completed till many decades later, it has a long and lofty nave beneath which Lord Edward Carson, the Ulster Unionist leader most closely linked with the partition of Ireland in 1920, lies buried. The fine mosaic on the baptistry ceiling is one of the high points.

SINCLAIR SEAMEN'S CHURCH
Corporation St at Corporation Sq. You would have to travel far to find a church interior as unusual as this gleaming shrine to the seafaring tradition. Completed in 1856—by Charles Lanyon, yet again—it is thought to be the only church anywhere built specifically for seamen and furnished with a plethora of maritime artifacts. The pulpit is in the form of a prow; the organ has the port and starboard lights of a Guinness boat from the Liffey in Dublin; the bell rung before evening service is from HMS Hood, sunk off Jutland in 1916; there is a capstan, a wheel, a shining binnacle, and even the collection plates are in the shape of lifeboats. Still a well-supported Presbyterian church, it is beautifully kept by a friendly congregation. *Services Sun 11.30 am and 7 pm; also open to visitors Wed 2–4 pm.*

CUSTOM HOUSE
Donegall Quay, and **HARBOUR OFFICE**, **Corporation Sq**. If you find yourself in the docks area, be sure to keep an eye out for these two fine buildings dating from the days when Belfast was a major port. The Custom House, currently undergoing major reconstruction, is one of Charles Lanyon's most splendid buildings—a weighty testimonial when you bear in mind that he was responsible for almost all the public buildings of note in Victorian Belfast. Grand and Palladian in style, it enshrines Britannia, Neptune and Mercury in its sculptured pediment, facing the waterfront. The nearby Harbour Office, already restored and floodlit at night, was built in 1854, in a slightly more severe rendering of the Italian style. It stands right beside Sinclair Seamen's Church (*See* above).

QUEEN'S UNIVERSITY
University Rd. Set back from the road in well-tended grounds, the long brick facade of Queen's University has a dignified elegance about it, especially at night when it glows in amber floodlights. With Cork and Galway, it was one of the sisterhood of Queen's Colleges established in 1845. The architect was Belfast's construction superhero Charles Lanyon, this time experimenting with a mock Tudor style which is said to be a remodelling of Magdalen College, Oxford. Unlike Magdalen with its series of beautiful quadrangles, Queen's is more appealing outside than in. Still, it deserves more than a cursory glance. While you are there, notice University Square, the handsome terrace which flanks the university's north side. Once it was Belfast's Harley Street, populated by doctors. Now all the houses, with their fine pillared doorways and fanlights, are university-owned. Dwell on these fine things and avert your eyes from the gruesome Students' Union building across the way.

GRANDEST OF THE BANKS

Waring St. Belfast's prosperous mercantile past is gloriously enshrined in two neighbouring bank buildings of extreme grandeur. The **ULSTER BANK,** designed by the Scottish architect James Hamilton in 1860, is a red sandstone conceit like a Venetian palace, above whose portico Grecian urns and the figure of Britannia flanked by Justice and Commerce are lined up against the sky. The former headquarters of the **NORTHERN BANK** is another flamboyant Italianate building, designed by the heroically prolific Charles Lanyon in 1845, and apparently modelled on the Reform Club in London. Look out for them if you are en route to the Tourist Information Centre in nearby North Street, and sigh for the days when banks invested in architectural splendour.

LAGAN LOOKOUT

Donegall Quay. Tucked in at one end of the new Lagan Weir at the centre of the Laganside redevelopment scheme, this modest circular visitor centre is the sort of place you might not

Queen's University

27

think worth a second thought, never mind a special trip. In fact, it is a delight. At the windows all around, landmarks and the history of the parts of the city at which they stand are brilliantly documented; you can listen to stories about local characters, and Belfast's engineering past is interestingly portrayed. Most impressive of all is the section on the ambitious weir project, completed in 1993 to keep the Lagan water level up and reinstate the rich wildlife pollution had destroyed. Across the river you look straight at Queen's Island, Belfast's shipbuilding soul. For adults and children. *Open Mar–Sept Mon–Fri 11 am–5 pm, Sat 12 noon– 5 pm, Sun 2–5 pm; Oct–Feb Mon–Fri 11.30 am–3.30 pm, Sat 1–4.30 pm, Sun 2–4.30 pm.*

BOTANIC GARDENS
University Rd and College Pk. When it was decided, in 1865, to allow free admission on Saturday afternoons to the Royal Belfast Botanic Garden, it was apparently not unusual for up to 10,000 citizens to disport themselves there at one time. Now, with free admission all the time, and the 19th-century passion for botany in decline, the gardens are rarely overpopulated. In fact this well-tended oasis of green between Queen's University and the river Lagan deserves to be much more widely enjoyed—not just for the children's playground and pleasant walks past colourful borders, but for two Victorian curiosities the Palm House and the Tropical Ravine.

THE PALM HOUSE is the earliest surviving example, anywhere in the world, of a curvilinear glasshouse. It was designed, as you might by now guess, by Charles Lanyon in 1839, working in conjunction with the Dublin ironfounder Richard Turner, who went on to build the palm houses at Kew Gardens in London and Glasnevin in Dublin. Reopened in 1983 after painstaking restoration, it is still well stocked with exotic species, some of them thrusting high up into the grand elliptical dome.

THE TROPICAL RAVINE, in a rectangular brick building nearby, is another repository of torrid exotica. Charles McKimm, curator of the

Botanic Garden in the 1880s, devised what he described as a new 'fernery', with jungle plants flourishing in a sunken glen. In 1902 a pond was added to accommodate the giant water lily, *Victoria amazonica*. The steamy home of tree ferns, cinnamon, camellias, papyrus, is an unrivalled Belfast hot spot, especially on a cool day. *Palm House and Tropical Ravine open Apr–Sept Mon–Fri 10 am–12 noon, 1–5 pm, Sat–Sun 2–5 pm; closes 4 pm Oct–Mar.*

ULSTER MUSEUM
Stranmillis Rd. When you go to the Botanic Gardens, leave plenty of time to step into the museum—a much livelier place than its severe classical front suggests. It's worth buying the colour guide at the door (just 50p), so that you can dip in and out of exhibits which embrace everything from the Giant Irish Deer and a giant bird-eating spider to linen-making and other local history. Otherwise, you follow a sometimes baffling sequence which spirals up through four floors.

Popular highlights include the Egyptian mummy Takabuti, ceremoniously unwrapped at a meeting of the Belfast Natural History and Philosophical Society in 1835 by a Co. Down clergyman; and the Girona Treasure—spectacular gold jewellery salvaged in the late 1960s from three Spanish Armada galleons which sank off the Co. Antrim coast in 1588. Also recommended: the gallery of Irish artists (*See* Best Museums and Galleries p 68), and an outstanding collection of 20th-century fashion in the Costume Gallery. There's also a pleasant third-floor café with Botanic Gardens view, and gift shop. *Open Mon–Fri 10 am–5 pm, Sat 1–5 pm, Sun 2–5 pm.*

BELFAST CASTLE AND CAVEHILL COUNTRY PARK
off Antrim Rd. From a distance, it is easy to see how craggy outcrops of rock have earned the name Napoleon's Nose for the Cave Hill—the promontory sheltering north Belfast. Close up, you are a Lilliputian, clambering up over Boney's immense brow and into the famous caves which might almost be his nostrils. Worth doing, all the same, on a fine day, for the 200 acres now known as Cavehill Country Park

Belfast Castle

include meadows bright with wild flowers, birds and butterflies, and there is no better view down over the city and Belfast Lough. The park's centrepiece is Belfast Castle, built by the Donegall family in 1870 when Queen Victoria's fondness for Balmoral had made the Scottish Baronial style all the rage. Ask at the reception desk to see the seriously underpublicised visitor centre upstairs. The meeting of Wolfe Tone and the United Irishmen, plotting rebellion in a Cave Hill cave in 1795, is documented, along with many other aspects of the area's history and wild life, and you may see more than you expect with the guidable and focussable remote-control camera positioned on the roof. Antique shop, bar and restaurant in basement. Excellent new adventure playground in the castle grounds. *Heritage centre open Mon–Sat 9 am–10.30 pm, Sun 9 am–6 pm.*

BELFAST ZOO
Antrim Rd. Not much further out of town than Belfast Castle is the adjoining Bellevue estate, originally laid out as a pleasure garden at the terminus of the old Belfast Street Tramway Company. Since 1934 it has been a zoo—one which has overcome a serious period of decline to become a fine example of what a modern zoo should be. For more information, *see* Belfast for Children p 95—but you don't have to be a child to enjoy a day out among the sitatunga, Pygmy marmosets and spectacled bears high above Belfast Lough. Shop and restaurant. *Open daily April–Sept 10 am–5 pm, Oct–Mar 10 am–3.30 pm (2.30 Fri).*

MALONE HOUSE AND BARNETT DEMESNE
Malone Rd. For a combination of late Georgian grandeur and what seems like fresh country air less than three miles from the centre of the city, the Barnett Demesne is hard to beat. On a site sloping gently down to the Lagan, the estate

was laid out in the 1840s by a prominent Belfast merchant, William Wallace Legge, who had the Belfast to Dublin coach road moved so that it would be out of sight of his new mansion. The bow-fronted cream facade of Malone House still dominates Legge's carefully landscaped grounds. Its last resident, William Barnett, breeder of the 1929 Derby winner Trigo, bequeathed the entire estate to the citizens of Belfast, who still enjoy its tranquil beauty. You will see it if you walk the Lagan towpath (*see* Best Walk, p 32).

SIR THOMAS AND LADY DIXON PARK AND INTERNATIONAL ROSE GARDEN

Upr Malone Rd. Further south but also easily combined with a stroll along the Lagan is one of Belfast's most beautiful parks, named after the estate's last owners. At its centre, Wilmont House, which once belonged to the Bristow banking family, is now an old people's home. It is the gardens which are the main attraction— especially the rose gardens, laid out for trials over 30 years ago at the instigation of the great Portadown grower Sam McGredy. Redeveloped and now rather grandly retitled the City of Belfast International Rose Garden, this wonderfully colourful collection of 20,000 fragrant specimens draws visitors all summer long: vast crowds arrive during Rose Week in July. There is also a Japanese garden, children's play area, shop and restaurant. *Open all year round, daylight hours.*

BEST WALK

With tourist board leaflets and information from this book, it's easy to devise a whole variety of interesting Belfast walks—pub crawls, Victorian architectural tours or whatever takes your fancy. But the loveliest walk of all is the sort you would least expect to be able to enjoy during a visit to a major city.

The Lagan Towpath takes you on a southerly meander through meadows and woodland, past old locks, under old bridges—and the only noise you are likely to hear is birdsong or the heavy breathing of a jogger. The long finger of countryside the river and the old Lagan canal bisect is a conservation and recreation area—the Lagan Valley Regional Park. The astonishing thing is that this rural tranquility—a real case of *rus in urbe*—starts not much more than a mile from the city centre.

If you are feeling energetic, you can actually walk along ten full miles of riverbank. For the more sluggish among us, in need of some enticement to embrace fresh air and exercise, the most attractive stretch is less than five, with the lure of a good pub at either end. With plenty of access points along the way (many with car parks), it is easy to choose an even shorter segment. Look out for the *Lagan Valley Regional Park* leaflet, which has an excellent map.

THE LEISURELY LAGAN SAUNTER

Start beside the river at Stranmillis, near the **CUTTER'S WHARF** (*see* Best Places to Eat p 38, and Best Bars p 49) on Lockview Road. From here you traverse the Lagan Meadows—120 acres of woodland, hay meadow, pasture where cows have grazed for nearly a century, and marsh where you may glimpse herons, wild orchids or yellow irises. On, then, to the five stone arches of Shaw's Bridge, named after a Captain Shaw who built the original timber structure in 1655 so that Cromwell's guns could cross the Lagan. From here the towpath passes by the Minnowburn, overhung with beech trees that blaze with gold in autumn, then skirts Barnett Demesne (*see* Best Places to Visit p 30). Another mile or two of twists and turns in the river, and you can leave the path at Drum Bridge. Go up on one side, and look down on the other to spy a sweet little lock-keeper's cottage, nestling in among hawthorn and willow.

Finish a few hundred yards further south, passing the pretty lych gate of Drumbeg church and taking the right fork in the road, at **ROBERT STEWART'S**, an old spirit grocer. Its refurbishment—wall-to-wall nostalgia—is a touch heavy-handed, but it's a cosy place with good lunchtime food. In the evening, it operates purely as a bar, and the most attractive part is also the most authentic: the public bar in at the back. Perfect—provided you don't have children with you. The licensing laws, dictating over-18s only, are rigorously enforced.

BEST PLACES TO EAT

The increase in eating out which typified the 1980s reached gargantuan proportions in Belfast, in spite of continuing political unrest. It was a defiant sign, perhaps, that people had been cooped up at home for too long and craved a congenial night out. So many restaurants opened south of the city centre that the stretch between the Grand Opera House on Great Victoria Street and the lower part of the Stranmillis Road near Queen's University came to be known as the Golden Mile. It still has the most concentrated range of restaurants at all price levels, with low-cost studenty places in indigestible quantities; but a number of restaurants further out are good enough to warrant a special pilgrimage, combined, perhaps, with a visit to somewhere interesting outside Belfast (*see* Best Trips Out of Town p 82).

What kind of food can you expect? With the arrival of Roscoff, probably the most highly acclaimed restaurant in Ireland, adventurous modern cooking has begun to make its mark in a way that earlier food trends like nouvelle cuisine never did. Modish Mediterranean ingredients like pesto, roasted peppers and sundried tomatoes are being sprinkled through more and more menus. But Belfast eaters have hearty appetites, and there's still a predilection for prodigious quantities of meat, rich sauces and cholesterol-challenging desserts.

Ice-cream is always in favour, as it has been in Belfast since the Italians set up their superlative cream parlours a hundred years ago. Although few of the originals remain, the tradition is maintained by one or two excellent places which ice-cream addicts of all ages shouldn't miss.

Be careful to check opening times before you plan your Belfast visit around a special meal. Some restaurants don't open on Saturday at all; others open only in the evening, and there are some which are open in the evening on Friday and Saturday only. Sunday opening is becoming less of a rarity than before. The other point to bear in mind is that Belfast people tend to dine relatively early—although there are signs of a trend towards later eating.

PRICE CATEGORIES

Price bands are approximate: à la carte meals can vary greatly, depending on the dishes chosen. Prices are per head excluding wine and service

Expensive
Lunch over £12, three-course dinner over £18

Moderate
Lunch £8–12, three-course dinner £12–18

Inexpensive
Lunch under £8, three-course dinner under £12

A treat from Roscoff: steamed Dublin Bay prawns wrapped in leeks with a sesame and ginger vinaigrette

ROSCOFF
Lesley House, Shaftesbury Sq, tel 331 532.
Paul Rankin grew up in Belfast, then travelled

the world, worked for the Roux Brothers in London and ran his own place in the Napa Valley before coming home with his culinarily gifted Canadian wife Jeanne to open Roscoff. It's minimalist-chic and California-cool, with its pale walls and blonde wood which some people seem to find too stark; but to serious food lovers it is quite simply the best restaurant in Belfast, if not Ireland, if not the world. In just five years, the Rankins have become big cheeses in international cookery circles, garnering awards and starring in their own TV series *Gourmet Ireland*. Even so, they still look after the shop, ensuring the deft execution of wonderfully exciting menus which use good local produce in season. Pigeon and wild mushroom bruschetta, for instance; roast monkfish with winter vegetables and a champagne vinegar butter; chargrilled Moroccan lamb with couscous and roast tomatoes—and an excellent, wide-ranging wine list. No wonder more and more Dubliners take the train north for lunch. *Open for lunch Mon–Fri, for dinner Mon–Sat. Expensive.*

NICK'S WAREHOUSE
35 Hill St, tel 439 690. Warehouse suggests vastness, a big open space. In fact, space is the thing you are least likely to find in this small, humming restaurant where there are two sorts of waiters—the pleasant ones dressed in green, to match the tables, and the glowering ones in the queue. Nick Price ran two popular restaurants in Co. Down before moving in among bricks and beams in this upwardly mobile part of town. In the downstairs wine bar—'still the only real wine bar in Belfast,' a blackboard proclaims—you can enjoy zesty, unpretentious food at unpretentious prices. Breast of chicken salad with fresh chilli dressing, creamy asparagus tart, beef and sausage casserole . . . Nick's inventive streak ensures a constantly changing menu, which comes with a good choice of beers and an exceptionally wide choice of wines by the glass. In the more formal upstairs diningroom, prices are higher, dishes grander—and the atmosphere more subdued. *Open Mon–Fri for lunch, Tues–Sat for dinner. Wine bar moderate, restaurant expensive.*

ANTICA ROMA

67 Botanic Ave, tel 311 121. The owners have had a huge amount of fun conjuring up the mood of ancient Rome in this restaurant like no other—a wacky assemblage of statues, temple pillars, bas reliefs and frescoes. The whole effect is so exuberant, so crazily over-the-top, that dining here is huge fun, too—the nearest thing to Trastevere you are likely to find in Ireland. You may notice a couple of big family groups, grannies and children included, behaving as if they were Italians. Under the gaze of frolicking goddesses and feasting Romans, everybody else grows similarly animated. The food is secondary. Some of it is Italian (e.g. black spaghetti with squid, cockles and prawns), some distinctly unItalian (e.g. pancake with salmon and parsley). Some is fine and some downright disappointing. The strange thing is that for once, it doesn't really seem to matter. *Open for lunch Mon–Fri, for dinner Mon–Sat. Expensive.*

SAINTS AND SCHOLARS

1–3 University St, tel 325 137, and **AUBERGINES AND BLUE JEANS,** same address, **tel 233 700**. It was to these popular sister restaurants owned by a Dutchman, Dirk Lakeman, that the British Prime Minister John Major was brought during a visit to Belfast, rather to the surprise of some of the city's grander restaurateurs. Drinks were served in ABJs—a casual café/wine bar with a cool continental feel and intriguing décor (the jeans of the owner and various workmen preserved for perpetuity on plaster torsos). Then on to dinner in Saints and Scholars—the quiet part upstairs, where the lucky few escape. The menu is eclectic—Cajun swordfish, Thai chicken, Languedoc cassoulet, and a lot of plainer fare: mixed reports suggest some unevenness in the cooking. ABJ's all-day food is funkier and cheaper, with a wide choice of snacks and special value before 7 pm. *Saints & Scholars open for lunch Mon–Fri and Sun, for dinner nightly. Moderate. ABJs open for meals, snacks, coffee, drinks, Mon–Sat 12 noon– 11 pm, Sun 12.30–10 pm. Inexpensive.*

MALONEY'S
33–35 Malone Rd, tel 682 929. Beside the perennially overflowing 'Bot' and 'Egg' (*see* Best Nightlife p 80), Maloney's was opened a few years ago to help bridge the gap between places like Roscoff, with cutting-edge cuisine, and Belfast's multiplicity of cheap eateries. It looks and feels like a bar-restaurant belonging to a reasonably upmarket American chain: bottle green paint, bricks, green and white checked cloths and a well-heeled clientèle. The food is substantial and a touch conservative (deep-fried mushrooms, bacon Caesar salad, pork en croûte), except for the Southern and Mexican menu which comes as a welcome change— especially to students who get a 20 per cent discount. *Open daily for lunch and dinner. Moderate.*

The Cutter's Wharf

THE CUTTER'S WHARF
Lockview Rd, Stranmillis, tel 663 388. 'A yuppie place,' non-yuppies are inclined to say of this big bar-restaurant down beside the boathouses on the Lagan. But on a fine summer's day, as you sip your drink on the terrace while the eights glide by, yuppiedom seems strangely pleasurable—and on less fine days, the red brick interior casts a rosy glow. It's one of those places where the atmosphere and

situation are more impressive than the food, which veers towards the pedestrian. Bar food served downstairs at lunchtime includes steak and Guinness pie and the ubiquitous lasagne. The upstairs diningroom, candlelit at night, has a bigger, posher menu: lots of steak, fish and chicken dishes and various calorific puddings. Jazz brunch in the bar on Sundays—a musical Ulster fry. *Bar lunch Mon–Sat; dining room open for lunch Mon–Fri, dinner Mon–Sat. Bar moderate, restaurant moderate/expensive.*

VILLA ITALIA
39 University Rd, tel 328 365. The constant queue outside tells you the most important things you need to know about this middle of the (University) road Italian place, whose rather grand big sister is Antica Roma (*see* p 37) and whose down-to earth little brother is **Speranza Pizzeria** on Shaftesbury Sq (*see* p 97). It is good value, popular, reliable, and you can't book. Style seekers may feel the pink neon lights around the windows and the somewhat garish stained glass leave something to be desired, but nobody is likely to quibble much about tasty pizzas and pastas for £5–6. For a pound or two more, you can be fancier (swordfish steak!) but not necessarily happier. *Open Mon–Fri 5–11.30 pm, Sat 4–11.30 pm, Sun 4–10 pm. Inexpensive. No booking.*

Villa Italia

SUN KEE
38 Donegall Pass, tel 312 016. If you like the plush sort of Chinese restaurant, with bouquets of fake cherry blossom and velvet chairs, this is not the place to go. If you want authentic, inexpensive Chinese food, and don't mind widescreen MTV-Asia in the corner, this is. Belfast's Chinese community, kitchen staff

from posh neighbouring restaurants and other late-night revellers come to the Sun Kee for food which sometimes looks dubious (Cantonese duck stuffed with prawns, for instance) but invariably tastes delectable. It is one of those places where it pays to throw timidity to the wind, along with the menu, and simply ask to have the same as the Chinese people at the next table. They are probably tucking in to baby spare ribs, off the bone, with chilli and salt; then monkfish hotpot, beef flank hotpot, rice and garlic bok choi—those tasty Chinese greens resembling chard. Owners of adventurous palates won't regret it. Unlicensed: bring your own bottle. *Open Mon–Thurs, Sun 5 pm–1 am, Sat 5–11.30 pm, closed Fri. Inexpensive.*

EQUINOX CAFÉ

32 Howard St, tel 230 089. It was only a matter of time until Kay Gilbert opened a chic little café as the natural extension to the shop that sells Belfast's most exquisite modern tableware (*see* Best Shops, p 53). This is the place to go for a coffee (it arrives in an Alessi cafetière) or a stylish snack lunch: pasta with porcini and truffle cream sauce, for instance, or a hot filled croissant, stuffed with smoked ham and wild mushrooms and served with salad. It's a miniscule place, artfully fitted out with red granite tables and slender metal and leather chairs—but you'll probably spend more time looking at the clientèle than the furniture. Foodie goodies (e.g. porcini, truffle oil) are for sale in the café shop. *Open Mon–Sat 10 am–4.30 pm. Moderate/inexpensive.*

CAFÉ ROSCOFF

27–29 Fountain Pl. At the time of going to press, plans are well advanced for this new bakery café selling all the wonderful Mediterranean breads for which Roscoff (*see* p 35) is renowned. Ciabatta, focaccia, walnut bread, sundried tomato bread and more can be bought over the counter or enjoyed on the spot, transformed into sensational sandwiches. Pastries and really good coffee are further enticements to linger in a bright and airy café with French doors to the street. *Opening late June 1995, Mon–Sat 7.30 am–5 pm with late opening Thurs. Inexpensive.*

BONNIE'S MUSEUM CAFÉ
11a Stranmillis Rd, tel 664 914. Bonnie Turkington was raised in the restaurant trade, waitressing through her teens in her mother's **Strand** just up the road. Now, right opposite the Ulster Museum and the Botanic Gardens (*see* Best Places to Visit p 28), she has opened her own café in the former studio of the great Belfast artist, William Conor—a lovely, lofty space, flooded with natural light or lantern-light: it stays open long after dark. All-day breakfast, soups, sandwiches . . . everything is tasty and homemade, including Bonnie's breads. Wine available. *Open Mon–Wed 11 am–11 pm, Thurs–Sun 11 am–'very late'. Inexpensive.*

MAUD'S ICE-CREAM PARLOUR
231 Lisburn Rd, tel 661 639. Belfast dinner party hostesses save themselves the effort of slaving over desserts by slipping into Maud's. There are always about 20 flavours of luxury ice-cream on sale out of a total list of 100, all made from pure ingredients in the Wilson family dairy at Gleno near Larne. Pooh Bear's, the honeycomb one, is legendary; Belgian Chocolate the next best loved and Guinness the most surprising! Children also love the violent pink Bubblegum. All quantities, from 35p cones to £10 gallon tubs. *Open 7 days 11 am–9 pm.*

BEST OF THE CHAINS

CHICAGO PIZZA PIE FACTORY
1 Bankmore Sq (in the Dublin Rd MGM Cinema complex), **tel 233 555**. *Open Mon–Fri 12 noon– 11 pm, Sat 12 noon–12 midnight, Sun 12 noon– 10 pm.*

PIZZA HUT
44 Dublin Rd, tel 311 200. *Open Mon–Sat 12 noon–12 midnight, Sun 12 noon–11 pm.*

BEWLEY'S ORIENTAL CAFÉ
Donegall Arcade, tel 234 955. *Open Mon–Sat 8 am–5.30 pm with late opening Thurs until 9 pm.*

McDONALD'S
24–8 Bradbury Pl, tel 332 400. *Open Mon–Wed 10 am–2 am, Thurs–Fri 10 am–3 am, Sat 9 am–3 am, Sun 9 am–1 am.* Also **2–8 Donegall Pl, tel 311 600.** *Open Mon–Sat 7 am–8 pm with late night opening Thurs until 10 pm, Sun 10 am–6 pm.* **Also Dundonald Drive–Thru, 919–23 Upr Newtownards Rd, tel 480 100.** *Open Mon–Thurs 10 am–11 pm, Fri–Sat 10 am–2 am, Sun 10 am–12 midnight.*

* BEST PLACES TO EAT FOR CHILDREN *See* Belfast for Children p 97.

* BEST PLACES TO EAT OUTSIDE BELFAST *See* Best Trips out of Town p 84.

BEST BARS

The new energy in the Belfast restaurant scene is spilling over into the pubs, many of which double as casual eating places. With the focus of social life shifting back from the fringes of the city towards the middle of town, bars beyond number have sprung up or spruced themselves up, with every available old stone whiskey jar, every antique Guinness bottle, seized upon in the sudden passion to recreate Victorian nostalgia. There is also a revival of interest in Belfast's genuine old Victorian bars; many are down the narrow alleyways known as entries where they were safely tucked a century ago when drinking wasn't a respectable pastime.

Serious researchers of the perfect locale for a pint should look out for the *Belfast Pub*

Crown
Liquor
Saloon

Walking Tours brochure available from tourist offices. You can use it to navigate your own way from coaching inn to gin palace, or to check details of one of the escorted tours organised by the Northern Ireland Tourist Board, tel 246 609.

The emphasis here is on bars that are worth dropping into during the day. Those that assume a special allure at night are listed (or re-listed: some of these are evening stars also) under Best Nightlife, *see* p 78.

NORMAL LICENSING HOURS
Mon–Sat 12 noon–11 pm, often with late opening Fri and Sat until 1 am;
Sun 12 noon–2.30 pm, 7–10 pm.

THE CROWN LIQUOR SALOON
44 Gt Victoria St, tel 325 368. Belfast's crowning glory among drinking establishments is a place of such dizzying splendour and panache that in it you feel intoxified even on a glass of Ballygowan. An architectural extravaganza built in 1885 (*see* Best Places to Visit, p 22) the carefully restored Crown is in the hands of the National Trust; and it is greatly to their credit that it still remains a lively, much loved Belfast bar. Close yourself into one of the carved wooden snugs, if you can. Drink in the atmosphere—all that decoration, the griffin guarding the door, the gunmetal plate for striking matches—and bask in the shafts of golden light that shine through the stained glass. You could stay here forever—except that somebody else wants your table. Lunchtime food includes champ, pies, stew.

ROBINSON'S
38 Gt Victoria St, tel 247 447. From a tourist point of view, Robinson's suffers at the hands of its more august and grandiose next-door neighbour, the Crown. Still, the 'theme bars' spread over four floors of a former turn-of-the-century pub, seriously destroyed by a recent fire, have plenty of devotees. These themes range from Victorian in various flavours to

American speakeasy, with Rock Bottom—a bikers' bar complete with Harley Davidson—in the basement. Lunchtime bar food downstairs includes Irish stew and sausage and mash; upstairs there's a hot buffet and an à la carte choice which continues until 9 pm Thurs–Sat. *See* also Best Nightlife p 78.

KELLY'S CELLARS
30 Bank St, tel 324 835. Here you have the genuine article—the oldest licensed premises in continuous use in Belfast. Founded in 1720, Kelly's Cellars is said to have been a popular meeting place for the United Irishmen behind the 1798 Rebellion—Wolfe Tone, Thomas Russell and Henry Joy McCracken, who hid under the counter when pursued by British redcoats. 'Cellars' is a misnomer: it's a two-storey building with a plain, stone-floored bar downstairs and a beamed restaurant with big open fire above. Lunchtime food includes homemade Irish stew (two serving sizes: man-size and hungry-man-size) and Black Velvet steak pie.

THE GARRICK
11 Montgomery St, tel 321 984. A three-minute walk from the City Hall brings you to this hand-some, well maintained Victorian pub. The gleaming mahogany bar, the well polished brass and the panelled wooden ceiling with its cigarette smoke patina give this mellow place the slightly theatrical air you would expect of somewhere named after the great actor David Garrick. The theme is picked up in the new Back Stage restaurant extension, with its models of play scenes and snatches of quotations on the walls. Extensive choice of traditional food—roast rib of beef, steaks etc.—in both restaurant and bar up to 6 pm.

MORRISON'S SPIRIT GROCERS
21 Bedford St, tel 248 458. Even purists who vehemently denounce repro pubs and retro bars have been known to linger on a padded leather bench in Morrison's, casting admiring glances at the battered grocery paraphernalia and the smoke effects painted on the ceiling. 'It's so well done,' they say rather weakly—and so it is. Modelled on Morrissey's, the famous Victorian spirit grocer's in Abbeyleix, this big 1992

Morrison's
Spirit
Grocers

newcomer is in a listed building—an old stationery warehouse whose steel supporting pillars add to the considerable atmosphere of the place. It attracts a smart crowd—media people (the BBC is across the road) and youngish business types. Interesting lunchtime food includes chicken tikka, chicken satay, good stir-frys. *See* also Best Nightlife p 78.

NICK'S WAREHOUSE

35 Hill St, tel 439 690. Because the food in Belfast's only fully fledged wine bar is interesting (*see* Best Places to Eat p 36), it's easy to over-look the fact that this is also a great place to go just for a drink. You don't have to have wine (although Nick's impressive list, supplied by a number of different merchants, and the wide choice of wines available by the glass may make it difficult not to); there is a full bar and a cosmo-politan range of beers. Best of all is the convivial hum of people enjoying themselves. *Open 11.30 am–11 pm except Mon (closes 5 pm), Sat (closed until 6 pm) and Sun (closed all day).*

THE MORNING STAR

17 Pottinger's Entry, tel 323 976. Down an alleyway between High St and Ann St, the Morning Star dates back to 1810 when it was the terminal for the Belfast to Dublin mail coach. Its finest feature is its green and red facade, with a flamboyantly spiky iron bracket supporting the sign above the door. Inside is pleasant, too, though: it's a pub with a lived-in feeling—old terrazzo floor, smoky ceilings and a horseshoe of well worn mahogany bar. Food (served until 8 pm) ranges from a reasonably priced lunchtime buffet to a gargantuan 24oz rib steak. American visitors and others accustomed to large slabs of flesh, take note: 'Bigger if you want but please give us 36 hours notice,' says the sign.

THE KITCHEN BAR

16 Victoria Sq, tel 324 901. At lunchtime on Fridays, this old bar, mid-way between the City Hall and the Lagan, serves up to 60 Paddy Pizzas—soda bread base, ham and toasted cheese—astonishing when you consider that The Kitchen is nearly as small as it sounds. Opened in 1859, it is low rather than high Victoriana—a simple place whose main adornment is a long line of lovely old lights above the bar. Pat Catney, waistcoated and proprietorial at the counter, says his customers are anything from binmen to High Court judges. Lunchtime food high quality at low price, e.g. the legendary pizza or bangers and champ for £2–3. *See* also Best Nightlife p 79.

THE DUKE OF YORK

11 Commercial Court off Donegall St, tel 241 062. A victim of 1970s bombings, the Duke of York has reemerged as a cosy sort of place, decked out with old pine fittings, old mirrors, astonishing quantities of old soda bottles and various bits of obsolete printing press which point up its proximity to Belfast's newspaper district. (Leading local journalists look down from the walls in a fine series of caricatures from the old *Northern Whig* of the 1970s.) If you're lucky you may be able to insinuate yourself into the single pine snug. Otherwise, mingle with the mixed clientèle—office workers, tourists, postmen. Lunchtime food, all homemade, has won a Taste of Ulster award. *See* also Best Nightlife p 79.

THE FRONT PAGE

108 Donegall St, tel 324 924. This upstairs pub, popular with journalists from the *Belfast Telegraph* and *Irish News* nearby, is not to be confused with McElhatton's, the much more basic establishment underneath. In décor, the Front Page is a temple to drink—a place where old pews, stained glass windows and a stage like an enlarged pulpit combine to create a church-like interior which is curiously at odds, in God-fearing Belfast, with the consumption of drink. Lunchtime bar food of the usual sort—chilli con carne, burgers, pies. *See* also Best Nightlife p 79.

THOMPSON'S GARAGE
47 Arthur St, tel 323 762. Up to the 1950s, the lofty space which is now one of Belfast's newest bars was a city centre garage belonging to Harry Ferguson, Belfast's brilliant tractor and aviation pioneer. In 1910 he won a prize for flying the monoplane he had built three miles over the strand at Newcastle—an event commemorated in a mural high up on the wall of a pub that trades on its garage past with old car ads and other motor-driven memorabilia. Bar food up to 6pm includes steaks, burgers and some trendier items like crostini.

THE CUTTER'S WHARF
Lockview Rd, Stranmillis, tel 662 501. In the summer, you can sit out on the terrace and watch rowing eights glide by on the Lagan. In the winter, there is the warmth of brick and wood and a blazing fire. But it is on Sunday mornings, all year round, that the bar of the Cutter's Wharf is busiest—not just medium-busy, but crammed to bursting point as customers flock in for the jazz brunch that runs from noon to 2.30—a live jazz band, yours to absorb along with an eyeopening Ulster fry. Lunchtime bar food Mon–Sat includes steak and Guinness pie and impressive doorstep sandwiches.

BEST SHOPS

Belfast has always been a great shopping city—a bustling commercial capital where retailing flourishes, spurred along by northern business acumen and the canny native instinct for a bargain. During the worst period of the Troubles, there was a move away from the city centre to newer shopping enclaves—in Bangor, Newtownards, Lisburn or the string of small boutiques along the Lisburn Road.

Even so, **Donegall Place**, the broad boulevard leading from the City Hall down to **Royal Avenue**, is still the main shopping area. It is here that you will find most of the familiar British chain stores—some of them housed more splendidly than they deserve, in the former premises of grand old Belfast department stores; places like Robinson & Cleaver, where once well coiffed ladies would ascend wide marble stairs to buy a new frock and have afternoon tea.

Off Donegall Place to the right, if you start at the City Hall, Castle Lane leads to pedestrianised **Cornmarket** and the new **Ross's Court** complex of shops and casual restaurants. Off Royal Avenue to the left is **Castlecourt**, a vast shopping centre with an enormous car park. Clearly signposted from the Westlink, it makes a convenient base for a city-centre shopping spree.

SHOPPING HOURS
are generally 9 am–5.30 pm with late night opening on Thursday until 9 pm.

DEPARTMENT AND CHAIN STORES

The Castlecourt Centre Royal Avenue, has branches of so many well-known chain stores that you might conceivably spend a whole day there and never see the remnants of Belfast's grand old shops–never mind daylight. Best among them are a large **DEBENHAMS** (great tableware section, and a bargain Ulster fry in the cafeteria), **T.K. MAXX** (discount designer wear, *see* below), **SPOILS** (houseware 'seconds'), **LAURA ASHLEY** (prettiness applied to women's wear and home furnishings), **PRINCIPLES FOR MEN** (good casuals), **THE GAP** (even better American casuals, and for both sexes).

Castlecourt Centre

Between here and **Donegall Place** you will find **PRIMARK** (fashion at bargain prices) and a big new **HABITAT** (in the handsomely refurbished Anderson & McAuley building—*see* under Interior Design p 54).

Donegall Place proper is the home of a new **MONSOON** (women's clothes with an ethnic flavour), a new **DISNEY STORE** (Mickey Mouse & co. stamped on everything conceivable), **BOOTS** (pharmacy, housewares but especially cosmetics), **C&A** (budget fashion for all ages), **MARKS & SPENCER** (familiar to all), **NEXT** and **PRINCIPLES** (affordable fashion) and **CABLE & CO.** (less affordable but covetable shoes).

In **Castle Lane** the star is **KOOKAI** (polished French women's casual clothes). Further on, in and around **Cornmarket** are the cheaper chain stores: **BHS** (clothes, home furnishings, good lighting department), **WOOLWORTHS** (best for cut-price confectionery) and **LITTLEWOODS** (low-cost general store).

DESIGNER FASHION

Belfast doesn't have as many major outlets for serious designer fashion as Dublin, nor indeed most major British provincial cities. What it does have, outside the city centre especially, is a large number of fashion boutiques. The two main areas for these are in Bloomfield Avenue on the Newtownards Road, and about a mile-and-a-half out of town on the Lisburn Road. The shops below are more centrally located.

PROPAGANDA
4 Arthur St, tel 310 251, and **36 Howard St, tel 326 938**, is the place for upmarket designer clothes with an outré edge: Dolce & Gabbana, Diesel, Destroy and Irish designer John Rocha.

BRAZIL
41–3 Bradbury Pl, tel 245 552, and **Unit 7, Donegall Arcade, tel 310 043**, a well established outlet for labels such as InWear and Episode, has recently opened a handsome **PAUL COSTELLOE** shop next to its Bradbury Place branch. (PC is stocked in lesser quantities in Donegall Arcade.) The Dublin designer favoured by Princess Diana has his smart, sporty clothes manufactured in Co. Tyrone; Belfast fans make regular pilgrimages to the factory shop at Moygashel outside Dungannon for bargains, tel (01 868) 722 291.

PAPILLON
60 Wellington Pl, tel 331 460, and **73 Botanic Ave, tel 241 191**, aimed at the over-25s, carries a wide range of internationally successful labels such as Rodier, Alain Manoukian, Radar, together with costume jewellery, shoes and other accessories.

RENEE MENEELY
5 Donegall Square W, tel 326092, has catered for decades to sophisticated customers of more mature years: Louis Feraud, Escada, Laurel.

T. K. MAXX
Castlecourt, tel 331 151, is the sort of place fashion fanatics can happily spend half a day in—a vast supermarket offering serious discounts on top labels. Rummaging may uncover anything from Armani, Versace and

DKNY to Charnos lingerie. Men's shirt counter a special magnet.

INTERIOR DESIGN

EQUINOX
32 Howard St, tel 230 089, has blazed a trail for over ten years, stocking the full range of Rosenthal china, gorgeous Orrefors and Kosta Boda glass, Alessi stainless steel, Georg Jensen silver and some more unusual design curiosities, e.g. Charles Rennie Mackintosh cufflinks. The latest addition is a chic little café (*see* Best Places to Eat p 40) and a café shop selling kitchen-enhancing items like truffle oil.

TOM CALDWELL
40 Bradbury Pl, tel 323 226, is an even older pioneer of serious good taste. Stock ranges from fairly traditional to strikingly contemporary: modernists will appreciate furniture by leading Italian manufacturers Cassina and B&B Italia; Italiana Luce's wonderful Dove light or the Nemo lamps designed by Vico Magistretti. There are also sumptuous oriental rugs, many of them from Iran and quite reasonably priced.

COPPERMOON
Spires Mall, Fisherwick Place, tel 235 325, is a contemporary treasure trove—a place richly stocked with wacky ceramics, clocks, mirrors in the stylish little shopping centre which has slid unobtrusively into the ground floor of the old Presbyterian Buildings, a pinnacled centre-city landmark. *See* also Best Northern Specialities p 61.

THE NATURAL INTERIOR
51 Dublin Rd, tel 242 656, is the northern extension of a thriving Dublin enterprise. As the name suggests, it specialises in fabrics an floor coverings made from natural fibres: wonderful Madras checks and stripes, coir matting of various sorts, and unusual curtain poles and tie-backs.

VIVID EARTH
93 Dublin Rd, tel 245 787, is another fairly new shop, filling the gap between expensive interior design goods and chain store dross with flair. An eclectic mix from Ireland and abroad, including Eastern Europe: colourful Bohemian crystal,

Vivid Earth | Polish ceramics, recycled Mexican glass. *See* also Best Northern Specialities p 61.

HABITAT
1–9 Donegall Place, tel 237 020, opened to such boisterous acclaim in the autumn of 1994 that within a few months it had extended its first floor. The chain set up by Terence Conran in the 1960s to breathe life and colour into stultified livingrooms is still brilliantly successful, bringing all the latest trends at unalarming prices.

BOOKS AND MAGAZINES

WATERSTONE & CO.
8 Royal Ave, tel 247 355, has a prospering outlet in Belfast as in so many other cities, with substantial and varied stock in all the main categories.

DILLONS
42 Fountain St, tel 240 159, is an equally popular and well established British chain; the Belfast branch extends over two spacious floors.

EASON & SON
16 Ann St, tel 328 566, is part of the wellknown and widely spread Irish chain, with an excellent popular range of magazines, stationery, books and maps.

THE BOOKSHOP AT QUEEN'S
91 University Rd, tel 666 302, holds sway in the university area, with textbooks (law and medicine particularly) and a good general section, specially noted for Irish history and politics, paperback fiction and the American Beat Poets.

GARDNERS
70 Botanic Ave, tel 323 146, sells all the familiar magazines, plus a great many puzzlingly esoteric ones. A small book and map section upstairs has a better selection of books on Belfast than some of the bigger bookshops.

MUSIC

VIRGIN MEGASTORE
Castlecourt, Royal Ave, tel 236 623, is the biggest and brashest outlet by miles, not just for music on tape and CD but also for videos (an entire floor), computer games, CD-ROMs and concert tickets.

THE GRAMOPHONE SHOP
16 Donegall Sq North, tel 240 046, is by contrast as long established as its name implies—a Belfast landmark which has survived the onslaught of chain store competition partly through its excellent location opposite the City Hall. Back catalogue CDs and country music are specialities.

VINTAGE RECORDS
52 Howard St, tel 314 888, claims to stock the largest collection of vinyl LPs in Ireland—every kind of music imaginable, from 1930s jazz onwards. Its sister shop, **GOOD VIBRATIONS 121 Gt Victoria St, tel 233 156,** also a specialist vinyl outlet, is more oriented towards current releases. Both are owned by Terri Hooley, godfather of 1970s Northern punk.

KNIGHT'S RECORDS
33 Botanic Ave, tel 322 925, is a popular family firm, much patronised by musicians, which turned from bicycles to records almost 40 years ago. Its main business is second-hand records, tapes and CDs, with jazz and blues predominating.

JOKES, FANCY DRESS AND FORMAL DRESS HIRE

ELLIOTTS
110 Ann St, tel 320 532, has underpinned the success of many a Belfast party for longer than anybody can remember. The business dates from 1886, has been in Ann Street since the 1930s and is still the city's biggest novelty shop. Werewolf head pieces, hand-knotted moustaches, luminous witches' nails—and dapper formal clothes for hire. *See* Best Shops for Children p 97.

CRAFT AND HOBBY MATERIALS

CRAFTWORLD
23 Queen St, 438 041, is a large and well-stocked shop that is sure to appeal to the nimble-fingered: everything from rug-making equipment, raffia and a wide range of ribbons to build-it-yourself models of all kinds.

JEWELLERY

FRED J. MALCOLM
18 Chichester St, tel 321 491, and **71 Botanic Ave, tel 326 793**, is a Belfast institution from the 1920s, far superior to the average jewellery shop in the range it carries and the oldfashioned courtesy with which it treats customers. Wonderful antique jewellery and silverware, and well designed modern gold and silver pieces, too.

ANTIQUES

The northern tendency towards neat, modern homes is perhaps one reason why Belfast has traditionally been a good place to buy old furniture and bric-a-brac. Real bargains are harder to find now than a few years ago, however. Southern dealers, attracted by the keen prices, have arrived in force to snap most of them up. But you might still be lucky, and as every antique addict knows, half of the pleasure is in the hunt. Head for **DONEGALL PASS** and the **LISBURN ROAD**.

Donegall Pass, Belfast's main antiques street, leads east from Shaftesbury Square. The best time to come is on a Saturday morning, when all the shops are open and two markets are in full swing at the far end. The best is the **BELFAST ANTIQUES MARKET**, upstairs above the fireplace shop winningly called Alexander the Grate. Here, 14 traders sell a good variety of wares, including interesting lighting fixtures, old postcards, advertisements, bottles and vintage toys as well as more predictable stuff.

Other Donegall Pass shops worth looking out for include **PAST AND PRESENT at no. 60, tel 333137,** for old pine and linen; **OAKLAND ANTIQUES at no. 137, tel 230176,** for silver and other quality items; **CARROLL'S at no. 82, tel 238246,** for furniture and **ZOOTER'S at no. 88 (no tel)** for vintage clothing.

Lisburn Rd

TERRACE ANTIQUES
411a Lisburn Rd, tel 663 943, has a small but interesting selection of jewellery, china and small household items. Also good for old linen: *see* Best Northern Specialities p 66.

MARLBOROUGH ANTIQUES
579a Lisburn Rd, tel 683 353, a recent addition to the antiques scene, has an outer area and an inner shop which between them provide great rummaging territory: a real needle-to-haystack place.

BALMORAL ANTIQUES
661 Lisburn Rd, tel 665 221, is a jewel of a shop with interesting china and delph, glass, jewellery, clothes and some furniture, all in good condition. Also excellent for old linen: *see* Best Northern Specialities p 64.

WINES

Serious winelovers ignore the wine chain outlets sprinkled liberally around Belfast and head instead for one of Northern Ireland's two exceptional wine merchants. A half-hour drive out of the city brings you to **JAMES NICHOLSON, 27a Killyleagh St, Crossgar, tel (01 396) 830 091**, whose extensive list is particularly strong in burgundies and the Californian wines of Mondavi. *Open Mon–Sat 10 am–7 pm.*

In Belfast itself, one family firm has fostered the appreciation of fine wines for over 40 years. **DIRECT WINE SHIPMENTS 5–7 Corporation Sq, tel 243 906/238 700,** run by Kevin McAlindon and his two sons, is a splen-did emporium in an old grain warehouse near the docks. It was here, centuries ago, that ships from Bordeaux unloaded their wine for distri-bution to the gentry, using Belfast as a back door at a time when relations with England were strained. Direct Wine Shipments also import from source, maintaining a strong relationship with wellknown producers like Torres, Chapoutier, Jaboulet and Bollinger, but also sourcing inter-esting newcomers. The result is a biblical port-folio, ranging from collector's items and peerless clarets to earthy Portuguese plonk.
Open Mon–Fri 9 am–6.30 pm, Thurs until 8 pm, Sat 9 am–5 pm.

Direct Wine Shipments

BEST NORTHERN SPECIALITIES

No matter where you travel, there's always an impulse to buy something to bring home—something to remind you of your visit. Belfast hasn't yet attracted visitors in numbers large enough to warrant the entrepreneurial mass production of mini-City Halls; and maybe we should be thankful. There are much better alternatives.

CRAFTS

The crafts renaissance is an all-Ireland phenomenon. Over the past few years, a dynamic new generation of Irish designer-craftspeople has emerged, producing innovative furniture, jewellery, ceramics and more with a strong contemporary feel. Some of the most interesting work comes from the Belfast area. You can see it in shops, galleries and, in some cases, in the craftworkers' studios, if you telephone in advance. Anybody seriously interested in the crafts scene should try to obtain a copy of the pocket directory *Contemporary & Traditional Craft in N. Ireland*, published by Craftworks (*see* below).

CRAFTWORKS
15–19 Linenhall St and **Bedford House, Bedford St, tel 244 465.** The membership organisation for the promotion of crafts in Northern Ireland has two addresses—one a spacious modern gallery with changing exhibitions and the other a shop where you can buy smaller pieces. Names to look out for: Diane McCormick for shimmering ceramics and Anne-Marie Robinson for wacky ones; Andrew Klimacki (*see opposite*) and Jim Dunlop for furniture; Janice Gilmore (*see* p 62) for rich embroidered jewellery; Debbie Thomason for metal jewellery with an ancient feel, Pamela Wilson for contemporary jewellery with Celtic inspiration. *Open Mon–Sat 9.30 am–5.30 pm.*

THE STEENSONS

2 Little Victoria St, tel 248 269. With 17 years of goldsmithing behind them, Bill and Christina Steenson are Belfast's best established modern jewellers. They sell their own extensive range and that of an interesting variety of other jewellers from Ireland and further afield in a nice little jewel casket of a shop.

COPPERMOON

Spires Mall, Fisherwick Pl, tel 235 325. This small shop is the repository of daringly inspired pieces by craftworkers from Britain and Ireland, north and south. *See* also Best Shops p 53.

VIVID EARTH

93 Dublin Rd, tel 245 787. There's some interesting Irish craftwork here, in among an eclectic collection that stretches round the globe from Mexico to Bohemia. *See* also Best Shops p 53.

STUDIOS TO VISIT BY APPOINTMENT

If you have admired a particular piece of contemporary craftwork somewhere and feel you would like to see a wider selection, it may be a good idea to try to arrange a visit to the studio of the person who made it. You will probably meet the craftworker and may even end up commissioning a special piece, which exactly meets your requirements. Do telephone in advance, however, to check that your craftworker welcomes callers and that the time you have in mind is convenient.

Here are just a few wellknown northern craftspeople whose studios can be visited. For a more comprehensive list, consult the Craftworks directory mentioned opposite.

ANDREW KLIMACKI

Monlough Workshop, 39 Monlough Rd, Ballygowan, tel 813 451. Trained in the famous John Makepeace school of furniture-making in Dorset, Klimacki makes superbly crafted pieces whose spare lines do full justice to the beauty of the wood he uses. The range includes magnificent big tables, Shaker-influenced dining chairs and the irresistible Adirondack garden chair.

Jewellery by Janice Gilmore

JANICE GILMORE
28 Cyprus Pk, tel 654 867. Pageant Jewellery, the company name, perfectly describes Janice Gilmore's unusual pieces. Her earrings and brooches are intricately embroidered in rich, Renaissance colours, sometimes incorporating tiny beads.

MICHEEN BRADLEY
20 The Esplanade, Hollywood, tel 422 541. 'The country is inside me and it just keeps bursting out,' says Micheen Bradley—needlessly, as nature is obviously the inspiration for her big, glossy ceramics. A platter piled with shiny leaves; a pot disguised as a perfect cauliflower; a dish with a bird or a butterfly perched on its rim: these are not things for everyday use, but very special pieces—collector's items.

LINEN

You only have to walk past the fine old warehouses of Bedford Street to remember that, from the middle of the 19th century until after the First World War, northern prosperity was woven on the looms of Belfast and the mill villages beyond. The valleys of Northern Ireland's two principal rivers, the Lagan and the Upper Bann, determine the shape of the 'Linen Triangle', stretching west from Belfast to Portadown, south as far as Banbridge and Rathfriland, and back to the city taking in Dromore, Hillsborough and Lisburn.

It was the Huguenots who brought their weaving skills to this part of Ireland at the end of the 17th century. When techniques for wet-spinning flax were pioneered in the 1820s, the linen industry boomed for a hundred years before decline set in—hastened, in the 1960s, by the arrival of easy-care fabrics. Soon, the stench of rotting flax which I remember as the ruination of many a childhood picnic no longer hung over the countryside, and the napkins every household had aquired from some relative in the linen business were consigned to a bottom drawer.

A few of the old companies have survived, however, and the cloth they produce is still unrivalled by any imports. With the current preference for natural fibres, linen is back in fashion—and there is a new appreciation of the cloth that shaped northern history in such a fundamental way.

Northern Irish linen

THE IRISH LINEN TOUR, organised by the Linen Homelands consortium, is the most enjoyable way to spend a day exploring the history of linen and perhaps buying some at the same time. You will visit the Irish Linen Centre at Lisburn Museum (*see* below), see a present-day flax farmer's scutching mill in operation and tour a linen factory in production before weighing up the temptations of the factory shop. The tours run April–Oct; advance booking essential. Contact the Linen Homelands at the *Banbridge Gateway Tourist Information Centre, tel (01 206) 23322.*

THE IRISH LINEN CENTRE at Lisburn Museum, Market Sq, Lisburn, Co. Antrim, tel (01 846) 663 377, is well worth visiting independently if you haven't a whole day to devote to the Linen Tour. Beside the old market house where brown linen was once sold, this new, well organised heritage centre provides real insights into the linen phenomenon, and you can see Ireland's last hand-loom weavers at work. It also has a restaurant and shop. *Open Mon–Sat 9.30 am–5.30 pm, Sun 2–5.30 pm, late opening Thurs until 9 pm; closing time Oct–Mar 5 pm.*

SMYTH'S IRISH LINEN
65 Royal Ave, tel 242 232, is the best-known city-centre outlet for new linen—not all of it, alas, from Northern Ireland, in much the same way that not nearly all the lace in Brussels souvenir shop windows is made in Brussels. The outstanding quality of Irish linen comes at a price.

SAMUEL LAMONT & SONS
Stranmillis Buildings, Stranmillis Embankment, tel 668 285—a weaving company with a long and honourable pedigree—has a factory shop where there are often linen bargains, as well as 'seconds' of the famous deep-pile Lamont checked teatowels. *Open Mon–Sat 10 am–4 pm.*

BALMORAL ANTIQUES
661 Lisburn Rd, tel 665 221, has antique linens at exceedingly fair prices, with pillowcases, teacloths and damask napkins generally in good supply.

TOP TEN THINGS TO DO IN BELFAST

1 **Look down on the city** and Belfast Lough from the top of the Cave Hill.

2 Take the guided tour of the **City Hall**.

3 Drink in the giddily ornate **Crown Bar**—Victoriana at its best.

4 See the **gold treasure** from the Spanish Armada in the Ulster Museum.

5 Treat yourself to a meal in **Roscoff**.

6 Book a show at the **Grand Opera House**—worth it just to gaze at the painted ceiling.

7 **Stand in mid-Lagan**, high up on the Lagan Weir, and see the new riverside take shape.

8 See the best of **contemporary Northern Irish art** in The Gallery, in the beautifully transformed Ormeau Baths.

9 Stroll through the Botanic Gardens to admire the world's first **grand curvilinear glasshouse**.

10 Go to Madden's in Smithfield some evening to hear the best **traditional Irish music** in town.

Bleach green near Belfast in the early 1900s

TERRACE ANTIQUES
441a Lisburn Rd, tel 663 943, is another good place to source magnificent old linens at magnanimous prices.

PAST AND PRESENT
60 Donegall Pass, tel 333 137, also often has some beautiful old pieces, including christening robes or nightdresses.

HOME BAKING

The Irish breadmaking and baking tradition has always been particularly strong in Ulster—perhaps because relative prosperity meant housewives could afford to experiment with more ingredients than in some other parts of the country. If you are lucky enough to experience it, an oldfashioned Ulster tea is an unforgettable feast of home-baked breads, scones, bracks and cakes. Sadly, it is impossible to recreate it with the flavourless items on sale in most shops (except for the products of the Ormeau Bakery which still maintains a reasonable standard). There are, however, one or two home bakeries where you can buy the authentic taste of Belfast to bring home.

JUNE'S
376 Lisburn Rd, tel 368 886, has the most delectable wheaten bread, wheaten and soda farls, Scots baps, potato apple cake and a dangerous array of fancy little cakes, all made in June Henning's bakery outside Belfast. Luscious take-away sandwiches, soup and stew also—terrific for a picnic.

WINDSOR DAIRY
4 College St, tel 327 157, and **181 Lisburn Rd, tel 666 047**, bakes an immense variety of breads, scones (try the cherry ones) and cakes that taste like real food rather than insulation foam. Excellent take-away food also.

Soda farls

BEST MUSEUMS AND GALLERIES

The news on the northern artvine is that times are hard. One gallery owner's theory is that Northerners in retreat from the Troubles have grown accustomed to travelling more; either they are lavishing the money previously put into works of art on exotic holidays, or they are simply not at home enough to come to exhibitions, or both. But with artist-geniuses like Basil Blackshaw, T. P. Flanagan, Brian Ballard and Ross Wilson still at home and at work, the northern art world isn't exactly moribund. There's a long, strong tradition for visitors to trace, starting in the Ulster Museum and ending in the commercial galleries which show the work of talented artists still in their twenties.

ULSTER MUSEUM

Stranmillis Rd, tel 381 251. Northern Ireland's national museum is such a splendid institution that it is included in Best Places to Visit (*see* p 29). Its collections range through local history, with the industrial past a particular strength; antiquities including the 700–800 BC Egyptian mummy Takabuti and treasure from the Spanish Armada; botany, zoology and geology—all displayed in a lively way.

Less well known is the fact that the entire fourth floor is a series of impressive art galleries. There are works by international giants (Henry Moore, Graham Sutherland, Francis Bacon), but more interesting still is the Irish section. The Belfast School of Art, established in 1900, played a central role in establishing a northern artistic tradition which has remained vibrant for the best part of a century. See it here reflected in works by Paul Henry, William Conor, Dan O'Neill, John Luke, Colin Middleton, T. P. Flanagan, Basil Blackshaw, and the Banbridge-born sculptor F. E. McWilliam. *Open Mon–Fri 10 am–5 pm, Sat 1–5 pm, Sun 2–5 pm.*

THE GALLERY
Ormeau Baths, 18A Ormeau Ave, tel 321 402.
The display of contemporary visual arts in
Belfast has taken a big step forward with The
Gallery's move from Dublin Road to extensive
and exquisite new premises. The old swimming
baths have been converted in the most
dynamic, modern way to provide four gallery
spaces for all the visual arts, with a strong focus
on multi-media: there will eventually be banks of
computers where artists can work. While
mounting major international exhibitions, The
Gallery continues to promote contemporary
Northern Irish artists energetically—both
established names like Basil Blackshaw, David
Crone, Micky Donnelly, and newer ones such as
Philip Napier and Alice Maher. Well worth a visit.
Open Tues–Sat 10 am–6 pm.

CRAFTWORKS
15–19 Linenhall St, tel 236 334. A streamlined
gallery has recently been created out of what
was formerly the retail outlet of the official body
charged with promoting Northern Irish crafts—
and a new shop has opened round the corner
(*see* Best Northern Specialities p 60). The gallery
is the place to view and lust after stunning pieces
by some of the big names—Andrew Klimacki's
furniture, perhaps; Finula Cunningham's
jewellery; Anne-Marie Robinson's off-the-wall
ceramics. Afterwards you can always seek
consolation by going to the Craftworks shop to
buy a mug. *Open Mon–Sat 9.30 am–5.30 pm.*

FENDERESKY GALLERY
5–6 Upr Crescent, tel 235 245, moving late
summer 1995 to **Crescent Arts Centre, 2
University Rd, tel 242 338**. Jamshid
Mirfenderesky is an example, perhaps, of life imitating
art. He left Iran to study philosophy at Queen's
University and ended up opening a gallery
which has established a reputation as an outlet
for the key names in contemporary Irish
painting. It is here that you will find the work of
Felim Egan, Barrie Cooke, Ciaran Lennon,
Patrick Hall, alongside a new generation of
artists. The present gallery doesn't do them
justice, but the airy new space at the nearby
Crescent Arts Centre will. *Open Tues–Fri
11.30 am–5.30 pm, Sat 12 noon–5 pm.*

Basil Blackshaw in his studio

TOM CALDWELL GALLERY
40–42 Bradbury Pl, tel 323 226. A pioneer on the Belfast arts scene for many years, Tom Caldwell still shows the work of established and outstanding Northern painters like Basil Blackshaw and Neil Shawcross, but there are also talented newcomers to look out for, including Leslie Nicholl and Liam de Frinse. A visit to this gallery is a double pleasure as it occupies the airy space above Tom Caldwell's furniture shop—itself an exhibition of modern interior design classics (*see* Best Shops, p 53). Soon the basement will be converted for one-man shows while gallery artists hang upstairs. *Open Mon–Fri 9.30 am–5 pm, Sat 10 am–1 pm.*

ONE OXFORD STREET

1 Oxford St, tel 310400. This gallery is a bit off the beaten track, but the new Laganside development will change all that. In the meantime, it is a pleasant space in which to see the work of young contemporary artists, most of them Northern Irish. There are some more established names, too, including Ross Wilson: hardly surprising, as he is the gallery's art director. *Open Mon–Fri 10 am–4 pm.*

BELL GALLERY

13 Adelaide Pk off Lisburn Rd, tel 662998. Nelson Bell's handsome double-fronted Victorian home is a delightful setting for the gallery which occupies most of the downstairs. He has been in the art business for decades— long enough to build up a solid stable of Irish artists at the more conservative end of the spectrum: the late Downpatrick artist George Morrison, Cecil Maguire from Lurgan, the Belfast painter Hector McDonnell, the Dundalk sculptor Sandra Bell. *Open weekdays 9 am–6 pm, Sat by appointment.*

EAKIN GALLERY

237 Lisburn Rd, tel 668 522. Belfast's old masters William Conor, Frank McKelvey and James Humbert Craig are sometimes to be found in this friendly family-run gallery where the veteran landscape and still life painter Tom

Carr exhibits. Tom Kerr and Norman McCaig are other stalwarts of the traditionalist school promoted by Brian and Shirley Eakin in adjoining rooms on two floors of a converted terrace house. *Open Mon–Sat 9.30 am–5.30 pm.*

OLD MUSEUM ARTS CENTRE
7 College Sq North, tel 235 053 & 322 912.
This multifunctional cultural centre, housed in a slightly down-at-heel Georgian building which was once the august headquarters of the Belfast Natural History and Philosophical Society, is oriented more towards the performance than the visual arts, but there are two exhibition spaces where photography is a special interest. The coffee bar is an added attraction. Telephone for a free events programme. *Open Mon–Sat 10 am–5 pm.*

BEST ENTERTAINMENT

Through the very worst part of the Troubles, Belfast institutions like the Ulster Hall, the frequently bombed Grand Opera House and the plucky Lyric Theatre kept going, so that the city miraculously managed to maintain its cultural backbone. Outsiders—Dubliners especially—are inclined to hurl accusations of philistinism at Belfast, but the charge is outmoded and downright inappropriate for the place that produced the actors Kenneth Branagh and Stephen Rea; the pianist Barry Douglas and James Galway with his magic flute. The Belfast Festival, internationally renowned for over 30 years, also knocks holes in the claims of the knockers.

With the arrival of the big MGM cinema complex on the Dublin Road and the general reawakening of the city centre after dark, the entertainment scene is livelier than ever. This section covers the cultural end of the spectrum, but it must be said that some of the best evening entertainment in Belfast is to be found in the pubs: *see* Best Nightlife p 78.

THE BELFAST FESTIVAL AT QUEEN'S, every November, offers such an abundance of cultural riches that it's well worth trying to plan a visit to coincide with it. To obtain a copy of the programme in advance, contact the Festival Office, tel 665 577.

For an instant overview of what's on at any other time of year, pick of a copy of the monthly newssheet *Artslink* from any Northern Ireland Tourist Board office, or check the entertainment listings in the *Belfast Telegraph*.

THEATRE

GRAND OPERA HOUSE
Gt Victoria St, 24-hour information tel 249 129, booking tel 241 919. Few theatrical settings are more sumptuous than Belfast's gilded and velveted late Victorian Opera House (*see* Best Places to Visit, p 23). It tends to favour productions from London's West End, with stars of screen as much as stage among the cast.

Ceiling of the Grand Opera House

LYRIC PLAYERS THEATRE
Ridgeway St, Stranmillis, tel 381 081. Founded by Mary O'Malley in her own front livingroom in the 1950s, the Lyric has long since moved to bigger quarters; but the emphasis is still on Irish plays, as it was in the old days when Liam Neeson first tried his hand at acting. International classics and ambitious contemporary dramas are also part of the programme.

ARTS THEATRE
41 Botanic Ave, tel 324 936. Drama features alongside music in the Arts Theatre's wide-ranging programme which has broad popular appeal: pantomime, comedy acts, late-night productions.

GROUP THEATRE
Bedford St, tel 323 900. Once upon a time, the Group fostered local talents like James Young. It is still the main forum for local drama societies.

OLD MUSEUM ARTS CENTRE
7 College Sq North, tel 235 053. The upstairs theatre here stages 'fringe' and experimental work, as well as performances by noteworthy local companies such as Charabanc, Point Fields and Mad Cow Productions.

EMPIRE BAR
42 Botanic Ave, tel 328 110. Every Tuesday evening, this popular bar turns into The Comedy Club, the venue for a night of biting satirical comedy that decimates sacred Belfast cows of all persuasions. Starting time 9.30 pm approx, but it's wise to install yourself with a drink around 8 pm to avoid the queue, or worse, being turned away when the place is full. No booking.

CINEMA

There are plenty of cinemas of various sizes dotted around Belfast. These are merely some of the best known:

MGM
Dublin Rd, tel 243 200 for programme information, 245 700 12 noon–8 pm for advance booking. A ten-screen giant in a big new complex which includes the Chicago Pizza Pie Factory.

MOVIE HOUSE YORKGATE
100–150 York St, tel 755 000. Eight screens, in the shopping complex down near the docks.

MOVIE HOUSE GLENGORMLEY
13 Glenwell Rd, Newtownabbey, tel 833 424. On the north side of the city, easily accessible via the M2; six screens.

QFT
7 University Sq Mews off Botanic Ave, tel 244 857. Queen's Film Theatre, attached to the University, is Belfast's most enterprising cinema, with a long established reputation for interesting forays into the unusual or the avant garde. Two screens. Late-night shows popular.

TEN BEST THINGS TO DO ON A SUNDAY

1 Breakfast late at **Bonnie's Museum Café**, among neat churchgoers and dishevelled hangover sufferers.

2 Walk the **Lagan towpath** from Stranmillis through the Lagan Meadows, at least as far as Shaw's Bridge.

3 Drop into **Sinclair Seamen's Church**, before or after morning service, to see a unique maritime museum.

4 Sample the **jazz brunch** at the Cutter's Wharf.

5 Or book an early table for Sunday lunch at **Deanes on the Square**, in a tiny Victorian railway station.

6 Then walk off your gourmandise on a visit to the marvellous **Ulster Folk and Transport Museum** at Cultra.

7 Or have a close look at Belfast's old masters, William Conor, Dan O'Neill and others, in the **Irish galleries** of the Ulster Museum.

8 Unravel the warp and weft of local history at the **Irish Linen Centre** in Lisburn.

9 Sunday elevation at any time of day: look up at the ceiling of St Malachy's Church—**miraculously ornate Gothic fan-vaulting**.

10 Curl up and read any book (previously bought—the bookshops are closed) by **Belfast's great storyteller, Sam McAughtry**.

MUSIC AND BALLET

Classical, opera, musicals, bands

GRAND OPERA HOUSE
Gt Victoria St, 24-hour information
tel 249129, booking tel 241919. The
magnificent Opera House (*see* Best Places to
Visit p 23, and Theatres p 74 above) assumes
its rightful role with the spring and autumn
seasons of Opera Northern Ireland, but ballet,
gala concerts and other musical events are
performed at other times.

WATERFRONT HALL
Oxford St. It deserves to be high up the list
because, when it opens in autumn 1996,
Belfast's new 2,000 seat concert hall will be one
of the most luxurious anywhere. If you are
visiting before that date, all you can do is
admire its circular form take shape—the
centrepiece of the new Laganside.

ULSTER HALL, Bedford St, tel 323 900. Since
1862, this has been Belfast's most dignified
auditorium, with splendid acoustics and a
majestic organ. It is the home of the highly
acclaimed Ulster Orchestra, and also a venue
for big-name bands on concert tours.

ARTS THEATRE
41 Botanic Ave, tel 324 936. Popular musicals
and music acts, country and western concerts
and other band appearances are all part of the
all-embracing Arts repertoire.

TRADITIONAL IRISH MUSIC, JAZZ, ROCK ETC

See Best Nightlife p 78.

BEST NIGHTLIFE

Bars, not clubs, are the hub of Belfast nightlife—bars which often have music, traditional or otherwise, and enough atmosphere to attract a crowd which may find itself squashed and hoarse by closing time. For a time, the Dublin Road and Shaftesbury Square were the epicentre of late night activity, but with the new MGM cinema complex and the new Europa the centre of gravity has moved citywards, down Great Victoria Street and Bedford Street. Most bars have late closing on Friday and Saturday, and close at 10 pm on Sunday.

BARS

MORRISON'S
21 Bedford St, tel 248 458. Every evening, Wed–Sat, Morrison's throbs to the loudish beat of blues and light rock played by some of Belfast's best bands (e.g. The Gents, The Dead Handsomes, Shoot the Crow). And, vast as it is, the place is usually packed to overflowing. *See* Best Bars p 45.

ROBINSON'S
38 Gt Victoria St, tel 247 447. The diverse bars that constitute Robinson's are always busy in the evening. There's folk music in Fibber Magee's Sat 5–8 pm, Mon 8pm-closing; live bands of various kinds in Spot Thurs–Sat evenings, and a rock band in Rock Bottom Wed. *See* Best Bars p 44.

MADDEN'S
74 Smithfield, tel 244 114. Marooned in the old market area of Smithfield, Madden's is the Belfast pub with the best reputation for traditional Irish music in an authentic traditional Irish pub setting. Impromptu sessions upstairs and down, most nights. Low ceilings, old gaslights and wood panelling all contribute to the bona fide atmosphere.

THE KITCHEN BAR
16 Victoria Sq, tel 324901. In the middle of town, Pat Catney's Kitchen is a popular place for traditional Irish music, played in the corner of the bar on Fridays 10 pm–1 am. *See* Best Bars, p 48.

THE DUKE OF YORK
11 Commercial Court, Donegall St, tel 241 062. There's music in some shape or form most nights of the week in the long room at the back or upstairs; Northern Ireland bands star on Saturdays. *See* Best Bars p 48.

THE FRONT PAGE
108 Donegall St, tel 324 924. At night, the red lights and church furniture give The Front Page a special otherworldly atmosphere. Live bands of different kinds play on the balustraded stage Tues–Sat. *See* Best Bars p 48.

Larry's Bar

LARRY'S BAR AND RESTAURANT
34 Bedford St, tel 325 061. Here is the routine, as described by a veteran. With a group on a night out, you arrive in Larry's after a few drinks elsewhere. You have dinner—unremarkable except for the fact that, by the time the main course arrives, singing has erupted. Then, some indeterminate period later when the puddings come, people are dancing on the tables. So infectious is the ambiance that even staid civil servants warble and wobble precariously to the strains of the grand piano. Hours—or days?—

later the patrons totter homewards, swaying still like sailors unaccustomed to *terra firma*. When life seems tedious again, they will be back. Booking advisable. £5 per head deposit required at weekends. Open Tues–Sat from 5 pm.

THE WAREHOUSE

Pilot St, tel 746 021. When the Rotterdam Bar, wellknown for its music, closed for renovations, it sent its customers across the road to these more spacious premises. Now The Warehouse is wildly successful as a venue for music of every sort (cajun, blues, jazz, Celtic rock and more). A no-frills place down by the docks, where you might not want to leave your car and it can be hell to find a taxi, but there's a bus to the City Hall and south Belfast on Fridays and Saturdays at 1.15 am. Bar open until 1 am Mon–Sat.

LAVERY'S

14 Bradbury Pl, tel 327 159. There can't be a young person in Belfast who hasn't at some time gone to Lavery's, if only to meet friends and go on somewhere else. It's a Belfast institution—an old Victorian gin palace, now largely devoid of historical or visual charm but still crammed to capacity, especially at weekends, with a young studenty crowd who subdivide into various subcultural groups in the different bars. There's also a disco, on the second floor. You don't have to be an A student to work out Lavery's nickname.

YE OLD EGLANTINE INN

32 Malone Rd, tel 381 994, and **BOTANIC INN, 23 Malone Rd, tel 660 460**. A few hundred yards up from Queen's, these two old student favourites which face each other have to be treated as a pair. So similar are they in spirit and supporters (along with the 'Welly Park', *see* opposite), that customers often stray between the three, risking sudden death as they cross the busy Malone Rd. The 'Bot', as it has always been lovingly known, attracts more of a young professional crowd than the relentlessly studenty 'Egg'. Both have discos, Wed–Sat.

WELLINGTON PARK HOTEL
21 Malone Rd, tel 381 111. The Welly bar, whose eager night-time customers invariably overflow into the foyer, is known as the Hunting Ground—something you may see as a plus or a minus if you check into the Wellington Park Hotel (*see* Best Places to Stay, p 17). It's Belfast's most popular pick-up spot, a natural late night progression for many patrons of the Bot and Egg.

THE KING'S HEAD
829 Lisburn Rd, tel 667 805. Opposite the King's Hall at Balmoral, a couple of miles out of town, this popular pub in what was once a rather grand Victorian villa dates from the early 1980s—before the retro-Victoriana virus claimed victims all over town. It's a cosy place in the evening, especially if you tuck yourself in by the fire, next to the shelves of old books in the Library Bar.

CLUBS

THE MANHATTAN BAR/DINER/NIGHTCLUB,
23 Bradbury Pl, tel 233 131. This tall, shiny fabrication of mirror, glass and flashing neon stands like a beacon in the middle of Bradbury Place, mainly attracting clubbers in the 18–26 bracket. Reports suggest robust doormen, and the patrons are not always models of gentility, either, but it's certainly popular. Open Mon–Sat until 1 am.

BEST TRIPS OUT OF TOWN—
NOT MORE THAN AN HOUR AWAY

Yes, of course there are others. Before anyone should feel the urge to fling this list from them with all the force with which Finn MacCool is reputed to have picked up a clod of earth from mid-Ulster and hurled it into the Irish Sea, simultaneously creating the Isle of Man and Lough Neagh, let me record that Co. Down is unfairly represented here. Armagh may merit a special journey for its planetarium, and Lough Neagh, indeed, for its new Discovery Centre. Even in Co. Down, there are other places to see—Rowallane Gardens near Saintfield, exuberant with rhododendrons, and fine old villages like Hillsborough or Moira with its cutstone houses and McCartneys' scrumptious sausages.

I still say these are the six best trips you can take out of Belfast. Depending on your inclinations, each one provides plenty of variety, combining places of enough genuine interest to merit a special journey.

1 A MUSEUM LIKE NO OTHER

ULSTER FOLK AND TRANSPORT MUSEUM, Cultra, Holywood, Co. Down. Even people who have visited this vast outdoor and indoor museum a dozen times still go back for more because, like all the best museums, there is nothing remotely fossilised about it. Since it opened on its splendid site overlooking Belfast Lough seven miles from Belfast, the Folk and Transport Museum has been in a state of constant evolution, ambitiously adding new bits all the time, and still it is only 40 per cent complete. It deserves at least half a day, ideally longer—and even then you may still end up with a gallop to the finish.

It's best to start with the Folk part, while you are feeling energetic, for walking is required to see both the brilliantly reconstructed town area and a whole assortment of rural dwellings, scattered over a wide expanse of utterly convincing looking countryside. It is the diversity of the buildings—from Sandy Row terrace houses and one of the oldest national schools in Ireland to farmhouses complete with animals and manure—that makes time in the Folk Museum disappear. You cannot but marvel at the painstaking care with which almost all have been brought here from different parts of Northern

The Belfast–Bangor Ferry in the late 1870s

Ireland to be reassembled stone by stone, then decorated and furnished authentically. Inside most, you will find a fire blazing and a friendly, well-informed attendant. But if you linger up at the flax mill or the forge, you may not leave enough time for the Transport Museum. Train

buffs should note that the Irish Railway Collection, housed in a mammoth new building, has been voted one of the top ten transport museums in Europe by the Association of Railway Preservation Societies. Other galleries house a cornucopia of interesting exhibits: early Ulster-built aeroplanes and motorbikes, and the futuristic silver De Lorean DMC 12 Coupé constructed in Belfast in 1982. There is also a poignant section on the *Titanic*, the Belfast-built liner which sank on her maiden voyage to New York in 1912 with the loss of 1,500 lives. A new Road Transport Gallery is under construction.

Easily accessible by road (the A2) or by rail (take a NIR Belfast–Bangor train which stops at Cultra). Restaurant and gift shop. Tel 428 428.
Open
July–August: Mon–Sat 10.30 am–6 pm, Sun 12 noon–6 pm;
April–June + September: Mon–Fri 9.30 am– 5 pm, Sat 10.30 am–6 pm, Sun 12 noon–6 pm;
October–March: Mon–Fri 9.30–4 pm, Sat/Sun 12.30–4.30 pm.

WORTH A DETOUR

CRAWFORDSBURN COUNTRY PARK, with miles of walks along beaches, over headlands and through quiet woodland.

BEST EATING EN ROUTE

DEANES ON THE SQUARE
7 Station Sq, Helen's Bay,
tel (01 247) 852 841. Adventurous cooking in an intriguing setting—the converted waiting room of a fine cutstone Victorian railway station. Crisp white linen and menus liberally sprinkled with truffle oil, wild mushrooms, pesto etc. Booking essential. *Open Sun lunch, Tues–Sat dinner. Expensive.*

SULLIVANS
Sullivan Place, Holywood, tel 421 000. The chef/patron has a Roscoff pedigree (*see* Best Places to Eat p 35) and it shows. Innovative and confident cooking, but inclined to be pricey

considering the décor is cheerful rather than chic. Coffee/afternoon tea are deliciously affordable, however. *Open Mon–Sat 10 am–10 pm. Bring your own wine. Expensive.*

SHANKS
Blackwood Golf Centre, Clandeboye, tel (01 247) 853 313. Trendy new restaurant and bar designed by Terence Conran, with fashionable food (in goat's cheese/sundried tomato/pesto/chilli idiom) and a good wine list. Golfers proliferate in the stylish wood/zinc bar. *Restaurant open Tues–Sat evenings only; bar open daily with interesting all-day menu. Restaurant expensive, bar food moderate.*

2 MAGNIFICENT MOUNT STEWART AND A TOWN OF ANTIQUE SHOPS

IN AND AROUND GREY ABBEY, CO. DOWN
A ten-mile drive from Belfast along the eastern shore of Strangford Lough is the starting point for an aesthete's perfect day out. Architecture, furnishings, horticulture, history and the chance to rummage through quantities of heirlooms: those are the inspirational ingredients.

Mid-way between Newtownards and Grey Abbey, look out for the long estate wall of **MOUNT STEWART**, former home of the Londonderry family, now one of the finest possessions of the National Trust. The original house was built in the early 1800s by the 1st Marquess. He was less well known than his son, Lord Castlereagh, Foreign Secretary during the Napoleonic Wars and the 1815 Congress of Vienna from which, amazingly, he managed to bring home 22 Empire chairs. In the late 1820s, his rich half-brother gave Mount Stewart the elegant, classical facade it has today, together with its huge, galleried hall (complete with painting by the famous horse portraitist George Stubbs).

The grandeur of the house is matched by the luxuriance of the gardens, conceived mainly by Edith, the 7th Marchioness, in the 1920s to take advantage of a warm microclimate. When the azaleas reach their peak in late spring, the Sunken Garden is breathtaking; by summer, the formal Italian Garden is the focal point. While you wander through 98 acres of greenery and blossom, don't miss the Dodo Terrace, with its bizarre collection of animal statues; nor the famous Temple of the Winds, an octagonal banqueting house built in 1785.

Clearly signposted on the A20 between Newtownards and Grey Abbey. Tea room and gift shop. Tel (01 247) 788 387/788 487.
Open
April–September: gardens daily 10.30 am– 6 pm;
October weekends only.
May–September: house daily except Tues, 1– 6 pm;
April, October: weekends only.

A few miles further on, the tranquil little town of **GREY ABBEY** has done its best to preserve its namesake, founded by the Cistercians in 1193. The monks would approve of the recreated medieval herb garden, worth strolling in after you have inspected what remains of early gothic windows, effigies and the wonderful west doorway. But Grey Abbey also honours the past with the highest concentration of quality antique shops anywhere in Ireland.
Open
April–September: Abbey Tues–Sat 10 am– 7 pm, Sun 2–7 pm.

WORTH A DETOUR

CASTLE ESPIE WILDFOWL AND WETLANDS CENTRE
Ballydrain Rd, Comber, tel (01 247) 874 146, with the largest collection of wildfowl in Ireland. Restaurant, gift shop, art gallery, woodland walks. *Open Mon–Sat 10.30 am–5 pm, Sun 11.30 am–5 pm.*

BEST EATING EN ROUTE

THE REFECTORY
Unit 4–44, Mill St, Comber, tel (01 247) 870 870. Up an unpromising stairway opposite a petrol station lurks this new and relatively

undiscovered gastronomic gem. Truly accomplished, exciting cooking and a very reasonable wine list far outdazzle the *nouveau pauvre* décor. *Open Sun lunch, Tues–Sat dinner. Expensive.*

3 TO THE END OF THE ARDS PENINSULA

PORTAFERRY AND STRANGFORD, CO. DOWN—WITH A TEN-MINUTE BOAT TRIP IN BETWEEN. The Ards is the crooked finger that shelters Strangford Lough—a soft, green peninsula of farmland, edged with beaches, fishing villages and the weekend cottages of Belfast fugitives. At the point where finger and thumb pinch together at the narrow inlet to the lough, the long seafronts of Portaferry and Strangford face each other, linked by what must be one of the fastest and loveliest car ferry trips anywhere. For the best special effects, travel in the Strangford direction at sunset.

Ferry travels daily in both directions every 30 mins. Tel (01 396) 881 637.

PORTAFERRY, always popular with Northern Ireland holidaymakers, has a new reputation as the home of **EXPLORIS**, Northern Ireland's aquarium. Only proper when you bear in mind that Strangford, with over 2,000 marine species, is one of the richest playgrounds for maritime wildlife in Europe. Here, in giant tanks, you can inspect a good selection, from five-foot conger eels to circling sharks. Small children enjoy prodding at starfish and sea urchins in the touch tank while their minders grapple with the revelations of video microscopes.

At the Rope Walk, Castle St, Portaferry, café, gift shop, playground, picnic area. Tel (01 247) 728 062.
Open
*April–September: daily Mon–Fri 10 am–6 pm, Sat 11 am–6 pm, Sun 1–6 pm;
October–March: daily until 5 pm.*

STRANGFORD attracts a steady stream of visitors to its great architectural curiosity, **CASTLE WARD**—an extreme example of marital disagreement cast in stone. When the house was built in the 1760s, its owners Bernard and Anne Ward came to blows over the plans. Nothing too unusual about that, but their compromise is intriguing: a house with the classical facade the husband wanted on one side, and the wife's preferred neo-gothic on the other. The clash of tastes continues inside, with magnificently appointed rooms in both styles. Below stairs, the restored laundry puts modern-day chores in proportion. Also drop into the barn that houses Strangford Lough Wildlife Centre, explaining the National Trust's nature conservation work. Castle Ward is a treat of a place—especially in June/July when its visitors don evening dress to attend the Castleward Opera Festival.

On the A25, 1¹/₂ miles west of Strangford. Shop and restaurant. Tel (01 396) 881 680.
Open
May–August: house daily except Thurs, 1–6 pm;
April, September–October: Sat–Sun 1–6 pm.

WORTH A DETOUR

KEARNEY, a pretty National Trust village of whitewashed coastguard cottages on a knuckle of the Ards' outer shore, three miles from Portaferry.

BEST EATING EN ROUTE

PORTAFERRY HOTEL
10 The Strand, Portaferry,
tel (01 247) 728 231. In an 18th-century terrace right on the front, this old hotel, prettily furnished in cottagey style, makes the most of fresh local produce, especially from the sea. Portavogie prawns, Ardglass crab, Murlough Bay mussels all star on both restaurant and bar menus. *Open daily for lunch and dinner. Restaurant expensive, bar moderate.*

4 NORTH TO THE GLENS OF ANTRIM

GLENARIFF FOREST PARK, Co. Antrim. It may be pushing things slightly to include Glenariff in a list of possibilities within an hour of Belfast, but the Glens of Antrim are simply too splendid to ignore. If time is short, you should just about get there in an hour via the inland route, but allow a bit longer and take the coast road if you can. Beyond Larne, you drive under an arch of rock, signalling the start of the Antrim Coast Road proper—a serpentine route along the edge of white limestone cliffs, constructed in 1834 and still spectacular for the views it offers out across the sea towards Scotland. The beaches are also eyecatching, with their mixture of white limestone and black basalt rocks as dizzying to look at as an op art painting.

The southernmost of the nine glens furrows its way inland from Glenarm, but it is lush Glenariff, with its tiers of waterfalls, that is the most dramatic. Turn inland at Waterfoot and drive up one side of the glen until you see the signs for Glenariff Forest Park. From the car park there are four way-marked trails, varying in length from half a mile to five miles. It is the blue three-mile loop, winding past three waterfalls, that is the most remarkable. But no matter which walk you choose, you will be rewarded with marvellous views down the glen to the coast as you descend into woodland glades and back up again to the starting point. Deep within the rocky gorges of the Inver and Glenariff rivers, humidity encourages the proliferation of vivid green mosses, liverworts and ferns, and wherever you explore, the sound of rushing water is soothing background music.

On the A43 Waterfoot-Ballymena road. Visitor centre, shop and restaurant. Open daily 10 am–dusk.

Glendun
Viaduct,
Co Antrim

WORTH A DETOUR

**CARRICKFERGUS CASTLE, Carrickfergus,
Co. Antrim**—an unusually intact Norman
structure, built by John de Courcy in 1180 and
garrisoned until 1928. Children enjoy the nearby
Knight Ride, a monorail excursion through local
history from 581 AD. *Tel (01 960) 366 455.*
Open
*April–September: Mon–Sat 10 am–6 pm,
Sun 2–6 pm;
October–March: Mon–Sat 10 am–4 pm,
Sun 2–4 pm.*

BEST EATING EN ROUTE

**LONDONDERRY HOTEL
20 Harbour Rd, Carnlough,
tel (01 574) 885 255.** Unlike so many country
hotels horribly defiled by modernisation, this old,
creeper-clad coaching inn on the seafront has
kept its character intact. Good, solid comfort and
good, plain food are the hallmarks of the bar
food, lunch, high tea and dinner menus.
Moderate/inexpensive.

5 MOUNTAINS, BEACH AND BUTTERFLIES—THE MOURNES

NEWCASTLE AND SEAFORDE, CO. DOWN

All summer long, visitors flock to Co. Down's biggest seaside resort, as they have done since the coming of the railway—except that now your eye is likely to be drawn away from the sweep of golden sand to flashy family leisure developments like Tropicana Pleasure Beach. By contrast, the Mournes which give Newcastle its aweinspiring setting are still as blissfully deserted as ever, provided you wander a bit off the beaten track, armed with a good map. It's important to note that most of the access routes into the Mournes are not public rights of way but across farm land, so dogs must be kept on a lead and property respected.

With 15 granite peaks from which to choose, most of them grouped in a compact area just seven miles wide, there are invigorating walks beyond number. My own favourite, influenced probably by childhood picnics, is the tramp along the Trassey River to the great scooped-out U of the Hare's Gap, and on, puff permitting, up the steep side of Slieve Bearnagh.

Even if you never leave your car, a day out in the Mournes can still be splendid. You can do an entire circuit, driving south from Newcastle to Annalong, then turning inland to the Silent Valley reservoir, on through the mountains on the B27 and back to Newcastle by the B180. The views will surely tempt you at some point to get out and breathe the fresh Mourne air.

THE BUTTERFLY HOUSE in Seaforde, seven miles on the Belfast side of Newcastle, can easily be combined with a summer excursion to sea and mountains, adding a fascinating extra dimension to a day at one with nature. Dozens of exotic specimens will flutter around you while various reptiles and insects (a Chilean rose tarantula, a giant hissing cockroach) snooze behind glass.

On the A24 at Seaforde. Formal gardens with beech maze also open to the public; restaurant, gift shop. Tel (01 396) 811 225.
Open
Easter–September: Mon–Sat 10 am–5 pm, Sun 2–6 pm.

WORTH A DETOUR

CASTLEWELLAN FOREST PARK, Main St, Castlewellan, tel (01 396) 778 664— internationally famous for its arboretum, begun in 1860, with different sections for different seasons; rhododendron woods and a new sculpture trail add to the interest.

TOLLYMORE FOREST PARK, Tullybrannigan Rd, Newcastle, tel (01 396) 722 428—one of Ireland's earliest national forest parks and still one of the most popular. Stone follies, bridges, arboretum and the natural beauty of the Mournes.

BEST EATING EN ROUTE

BUCK'S HEAD INN
77 Main St, Dundrum, tel (01 396) 751 868. This smartly converted place on the main Belfast–Newcastle Rd has a cosy front bar with open fire and more formal conservatory diningroom. Fresh local ingredients (including Dundrum oysters and mussels) are competently handled in a wide-ranging menu extending from bar snacks to full dinner. *Open daily for lunch and dinner. Moderate/inexpensive.*

6 FUN FOR ALL THE FAMILY

BANGOR, CO. DOWN For as long as anybody can remember, Bangor has been Belfast's nearest seaside resort of serious proportions. In Victorian times, when terraces of genteel guest houses were built along its promenades, it was a lot more sedate than it is now, with its glitzy new marina and big shopping malls; but if it's family entertainment you are after, rain, hail or shine and to hell with the glitz, Bangor can be hard to beat.

The most recent attraction, right beside the marina, is **PICKIE FAMILY FUN PARK**—a sort of multiple choice open-air leisure centre along American lines. Children enjoy gliding across the Boating Lagoon in a swan pedal boat, working on their bravado in the adventure playground or chugging round the park in the Pickie Puffer train to the amphitheatre where there is a full programme of children's entertainment through the summer. Bangor also has more traditional outdoor attractions, like **CASTLE PARK** with its nature trail, and **WARD PARK**, whose year-round population includes exotic birds as well as migrant visitors.

If the weather does its worst, there is ten-pin bowling to try on a computerised 16-lane alley at the **CINEPLEX CENTRE**, which also has four cinemas and **MOWGLI'S ADVENTURELAND** for young explorers—or the prospect of a spree in **BLOOMFIELD** shopping centre. The more intellectual pleasures of **BANGOR ABBEY** and the **NORTH DOWN HERITAGE CENTRE** behind the town hall (with first-rate café) should silence any eggheads. And, oh yes, there is *one* good oldfashioned sea-side attraction. The beach at **BALLYHOLME**.

Bangor is on the A2, the main route east out of the city along Belfast Lough. Fun park on the Promenade. Tel (01 247) 270 069.
Open
Easter–September: daily 10 am–10 pm;
October–March: Sat–Sun only 10 am–sunset.

BEST EATING EN ROUTE

THE GRAPEVINE
Main St, Conlig, Bangor, tel (01 247) 820 219.
Two miles outside Bangor on the Newtownards
road, this relaxed, civilised coffee shop/
restaurant is the ideal place to bring children for
lunch or a snack that looks and tastes better
than anything from the town's fast food outlets.
Homemade lasagne, quiche, etc. Non-licensed.
Open Mon–Sat 9 am–5 pm. Inexpensive.

THE BAY TREE
**Audley Court, 118 High St, Holywood,
tel 426 414**. Good soup and light savoury dishes
make this a popular lunch spot, but it is Sue
Farmer's wonderfully sticky cakes that turn
normally restrained adults into greedy children at
any time of day. Both coffee shop and well
stocked pottery shop. *Open Mon–Sat 10 am–
4.30 pm. Inexpensive.*

MAUD'S ICE-CREAM PARLOUR
57 High St, Bangor, tel (01 247) 270 010. A day
at the seaside isn't worth its salt without a decent
ice-cream cone, and the Bangor outlet of the
famous Northern dairy ice-cream company has
the best in town. *Open Mon–Thurs 12 noon–
9 pm, Fri–Sun 10 am–10 pm.*

Bangor,
Co. Down

BELFAST FOR CHILDREN—
AND TEENAGERS!

With more and more child-friendly restaurants, child-focused tourist attractions, leisure centres and adventure playgrounds, Belfast is becoming a better place for young people all the time. The one place children and young teenagers are not welcome is in pubs, where the over-18s licensing law is strictly adhered to—even for toddlers wanting nothing more lethal than a glass of orange juice.

BEST OUTINGS

THE ULSTER MUSEUM
Stranmillis Rd, tel 381 251. There is something to interest young people of all ages in Northern Ireland's national museum. The hands-on presentations in the natural history section, the working water wheel, the Armada treasure and the Egyptian mummy are all tried and tested favourites. *Open Mon–Fri 10 am–5 pm, Sat 1–5 pm, Sun 2–5 pm. See* Best Places to Visit p 29.

BELFAST ZOO
Antrim Rd, tel 776 277. It used to be called Bellevue—an apt name, for the zoo sits up under the Cave Hill, facing the magnificent panorama of Belfast Lough. To its credit, Belfast City Council has spent 15 years and £10 million transforming what was once the sad habitat of threadbare animals into a shining example. Set in beautifully landscaped and well tended parkland, Belfast Zoo keeps an intriguing collection of animals in a relatively natural environment. Many are endangered species, participating in various international conservation and breeding programmes. Lemurs, tamarins and marmosets are a speciality—and the perennially popular penguins were all hand-reared in Belfast from eggs sent from the Falkland Islands. Lively brochures, maps and information boards make a zoo trip that is highly educational as well as enjoyable. Ark Restaurant

and Mountain Tea House, also picnic tables. *Open daily 10 am–5 pm Apr–Sept, 10 am– 3.30 pm Oct–Mar (closing 2.30 pm Fri).*

THE LAGAN LOOKOUT
Donegall Quay, tel 311 944. Slightly older children enjoy this visitor centre which explains both the engineering feat involved in building the Lagan Weir right outside, and the highlights of Belfast's mercantile and industrial past. *Open Mar–Sept Mon–Fri 11 am–5 pm, Sat 12 noon– 5 pm, Sun 2–5 pm; Oct–Feb Mon–Fri 11.30 am– 3.30 pm, Sat 1–4.30 pm, Sun 2–4.30 pm.* See Best Places to Visit p 27.

THE SUPERBOWL
4 Clarence St West, tel 331 466. This 20-lane bowling centre—the only one in the middle of town—isn't just for kids, but it is one place where most Belfast parents feel they can leave young teenagers for a few hours in the evening without having to worry. Four lanes are specially converted for use by younger children and the disabled, and Saturday mornings are specially for the under-12s. Video games room, restaurant. Booking advisable, especially for evenings. *Open Mon–Sat 10 am–midnight; Sun 12 noon–midnight.*

DUNDONALD INTERNATIONAL ICE BOWL
111 Old Dundonald Rd, tel 482 611. An Olympic-size ice rink, a 30-lane ten-pin bowling alley and Indianaland, an indoor adventure play area, are all combined in this vast leisure centre four miles out of the city. Special Saturday and Sunday morning skating sessions for young families, 10–12.30, while the bowling side of the house runs the Boredom Busters Club on Saturday mornings for under-12s. Restaurant. *Open Mon–Thurs 2–11.30 pm, Fri–Sun and all holidays 10 am–11.30 pm.*

BEST SHOPS FOR KIDS

THE DISNEY STORE
Unit 1, Donegall Pl, tel 246 477. To judge from the sweatshirts, large as well as small, and ties with the Seven Dwarfs tumbling down them, some very large children knock as much fun out of Mickey Mouse commercialism as small ones

do. Dizzying array of Disney items, from fluffy pink Minnie slippers to Winnie the Pooh bubble bath.

ELLIOTTS
110–112 Ann St, tel 320 532. An Aladdin's Cave of fancy dress, jokes, novelties, 'for children of all ages from 2 to 92', says the manager. All the usual outfits and accoutrements plus some more freakish items, e.g. Biggles latex flying hat and huge moustache, or a pink girl ghost outfit. *See* Best Shops p 56.

BEST EATING OUT

There is such a wide selection of casual restaurants and fast food outlets that no child need ever risk starvation in Belfast—and no parent penury. These are the ones most likely to be classified as cool.

CHICAGO PIZZA PIE FACTORY
1 Bankmore Sq (in the MGM Cinema complex, Dublin Rd), tel 233 555. All ages approve. A children's set menu at around £3 for pizza or other main course, ice-cream and soft drink; on Sundays, a clown or magician goes around the tables before staging a lunchtime show—and in spite of all that, teenagers love the atmosphere. *Open daily from 12 noon. No booking.*

AUBERGINES & BLUE JEANS
1 University St, tel 233 700. Dirk Lakeman keeps a big basket of books, crayons and games in his hip new café-restaurant so that parents can relax. No special children's menu, probably because the main one has burgers, spaghetti bolognese, garlic bread and other things kids like, including milkshakes. *Open daily from 12 noon. No booking. See* Best Places to Eat p 37.

SPERANZA PIZZERIA
16–17 Shaftesbury Sq, tel 230 213. This sibling of **Villa Italia** (*see* Best Places to Eat p 39) offers even better value, with 13 sort of pizzas for children to share at around £3–5, and a reasonable children's menu with other old reliables like chicken nuggets and lasagne. Steak and more substantial dishes for pizza-fatigued parents. *Open Mon–Sat, evenings only. No booking.*

J. J. BLEEKERS

42 Malone Rd, tel 663 114. An American-themed restaurant, lined with memorabilia, where parents can enjoy ribs or chicken smoked over hickory, adult-size burgers and the bounty of a full bar while children tuck in to the sort of stuff they tend to prefer. Children's set meal under £5. Puzzles, drawing materials and a competition to enter. *Open Mon–Sat 5–10.30 pm, Sun 4–10 pm.*

BISHOP'S

34 Bradbury Pl, tel 311 827. A newish fish and chip place with a pleasant, old-fashioned feel generated by tiled walls and wooden booths. Children's menu extends beyond fish to sausages, burgers. Open daily. Booking optional. *Open Mon–Sat 10.30 am–11 pm, Sun 11 am–10 pm.*

BARNAM'S WORLD OF ICE-CREAM

587 Lisburn Rd, tel 682 383. Just opposite Cranmore Park (*see below*, Best Playgrounds), a large illuminated cone attracts young devotees of superlative ice-cream. Many with palates attuned to the subtleties of homemade raspberry ripple and chocolate chip drop in to cool off with a high-rise cornet after a hectic ses-sion on the swings. *Open 7 days 10 am–10 pm.*

BEST PLAYGROUNDS

BELFAST CASTLE

off the **Antrim Rd**, has a new adventure playground in its extensive grounds overlooking Belfast Lough. *See* Best Places to Visit p 29.

BOTANIC GARDENS

University Rd and College Pk, has a corner near the Lagan where children can play after parents have admired the great Victorian glasshouse. *See* Best Places to Visit p 28.

SIR THOMAS AND LADY DIXON PARK INTERNATIONAL ROSE GARDEN

Upr Malone Rd, has a pleasant, grassy play area. *See* Best Places to Visit p 31.

CRANMORE PARK

Lisburn Rd at Cranmore Pk, has an adventure play area as well as the usual swings etc.

BEST EXPEDITIONS OUT OF BELFAST

THE ULSTER FOLK AND TRANSPORT MUSEUM

Cultra, Holywood, Co. Down, tel 428 428. The sheer scale of the place gives children plenty of scope to work of excess energy as they move from place to place, picking out the things they want to see. The vintage vehicles in the Transport galleries are always a hit, as are train rides on the miniature railway (Easter–Sept, Sat afternoons, public holidays). But children also enjoy speculating on the discomforts of life long ago as they inspect spartan dwellings in the Folk Museum, clambering up ladders to their young ancestors' sleeping quarters. *See* Best Trips Out of Town p 82.

EXPLORIS

Rope Walk, Castle St, Portaferry, Co. Down, tel (01 247) 728 062. Young people of all ages leap, dolphin-like, at the chance to have a fish-eye view of life in the Irish Sea at Northern Ireland's only public aquarium. Small fry like stepping inside the Shoaling Ring to stand among hundreds of writhing, glistening bodies, or poking at various creatures in the Touch Tank; but there is enough serious scientific information to intrigue older siblings also—especially if they are immersed in a school project. *See* Best Trips Out of Town p 87.

PICKIE FAMILY FUN PARK and **CINEPLEX** with its bowling alley and **MOWGLI'S ADVENTURE-LAND, Bangor, Co. Down**. These are just some of the highlights: the truth is that the popular old seaside town of Bangor is one giant new activity centre, geared towards family entertainment. It's not in the Disney World league, and toffee-nosed daddies and mummies have been known to lament its proletarian air—usually until their once-bored offspring turn suddenly exuberant and change their minds. *See* Best Trips Out of Town p 93.

TRACING YOUR ULSTER ANCESTORS

More and more descendants of emigrants, particularly to Australia, New Zealand, South Africa, Canada and the United States, are interested in discovering their Irish roots—and on-the-spot genealogical research may provide the perfect excuse for a visit to Belfast. It is a good idea, however, to do as much digging as possible well in advance. Get in touch with relatives, look through old family papers and letters and try to assemble as much information as you can. If you are lucky and a fairly detailed picture emerges, you may be able to find your ancestral home without too much difficulty.

If, on the other hand, your information is sketchy and there are unbridgeable gaps, there are a number of sources to which you may turn for help. You may save precious holiday time by contacting some of these by letter several months before your trip.

GENERAL REGISTER OFFICE
Oxford House, 49 Chichester St, Belfast BT1 4HL, tel (01 232) 252 000. Records of all births and deaths since 1864 and copies of all marriage registrations in Northern Ireland since 1922 are held here, and it is possible to obtain copies either by post or in person for a small fee. Central records prior to 1922 are held in Dublin but the General Register Office in Belfast can arrange for searches to be made of any births, marriages or deaths before that date—again for a modest fee. *Open Mon–Fri 9.30 am–4 pm.*

**PUBLIC RECORD OFFICE OF NORTHERN
IRELAND (PRONI)
66 Balmoral Ave, Belfast BT9 6NY, tel (01 232)
661 621**. This is a main source of manuscript
information for genealogical research—but only
for those who are able to come along and sift
through the records themselves. No fee. *Open
Mon–Fri 9.15 am–4.45 pm.*

**ULSTER HERITAGE CENTRE
64 Wellington Pl, Belfast BT1 6GE, tel
(01 232) 235 392**. Here, under one roof, you will
find the Ulster Historical Society, which carries
out research on a commission basis (typical time
required 4–6 months, typical fee £100–150); a
walk-in centre which offers genealogical advice
relating to the nine northern counties and a
service which collates church records—mostly
19th-century—relating to Antrim, Down and the
city of Belfast; and a bookshop with a wide range
of publications on genealogy. *Open Mon–Fri
9.30 am–5.30 pm, Sat 10 am–4 pm.*

BELFAST FOR CONFERENCE AND BUSINESS VISITORS

Like major cities everywhere, Belfast is marketing itself as an ideal conference venue—an initiative that is succeeding in the new, positive atmosphere peace has brought. Belfast is a good centre for national and international business meetings. Access is easy: by air, sea, rail, road. Facilities are impressive and improving: an increasing number of hotels are well geared to conference business, and the massive new Belfast Conference Centre and Concert Hall, linked to a new Hilton Hotel, opens in the autumn of 1996.

For the non-working part of the programme, Belfast has a vibrant cultural and entertainment scene (*see* Best Entertainment, p 73, and Best Nightlife, p 78), and the chunk of Northern Ireland on the city's doorstep offers genuine variety (*see* Best Trips Out of Town, p 82). A little further afield, the Giant's Causeway, golf at Royal Portrush, a 'wee Bush' at Old Bushmills Distillery or a balloon flight across the Fermanagh lakes are other enticements.

THE NORTHERN IRELAND CONFERENCE BUREAU
St Anne's Court, 59 North St, Belfast BT1 1NB, tel (01 232) 315 513, fax (01 232) 315 544, is the place to contact if you want to find out more about conference possibilities. You will be sent an extremely handsome and comprehensive brochure with details of venues and the bureau's service which includes advice on all arrangements, familiarisation visits, multilingual tourist guides, delegate welcome packs and much more.

MAIN VENUES

KING'S HALL EXHIBITION AND CONFERENCE CENTRE
Balmoral, tel (01 232) 665 225, fax (01 232) 661 264. Northern Ireland's largest venue, 3 miles from the city centre at the M1 motorway exit. The King's Hall accommodates up to 5,000; the adjoining Balmoral Conference Centre up to 600. Fax/photocopy/secretarial services. Accommodation in nearby hotels.

BELFAST INTERNATIONAL AIRPORT CONFERENCE & BUSINESS CENTRE
tel (01 849) 422 888 ext 2323, fax (01 849) 452 084. Easily reached from both the arrivals and departures concourses; 4 meeting rooms accommodate up to 130 people. Fax/photocopy/secretarial/ interpreting services on request. Accommodation in nearby hotels.

EUROPA HOTEL
Gt Victoria St, tel (01 232) 327 000, fax (01 232) 327 800. The most comprehensive conference facilities so far in the heart of Belfast, in a four-star hotel with self-contained business centre. 10 meeting room combinations accommodate up to 1,000. 183 bedrooms. Fax/photocopy/secretarial services. *See* also Best Places to Stay p 17.

BEECHLAWN HOUSE HOTEL
Dunmurry Lane, tel (01 232) 612 974, fax (01 232) 623 601. Three-star hotel on the edge of Belfast, 5 miles from the centre and airport, with two golf courses and a riding school nearby. 8 meeting rooms accommodate up to 350. 34 bedrooms. Fax/photocopy facilities.

DUKES HOTEL
65–67 University St, tel (01 232) 236 666, fax (01 232) 237 177. Bright, modern three-star hotel within Victorian building near Queen's University, Ulster Museum etc. 4 meeting rooms accommodate up to 150. 21 bedrooms. Small gym and saunas. Fax/photocopy/secretarial services. *See* also Best Places to Stay p 17.

STORMONT HOTEL AND CONFEX CENTRE
587 Upr Newtownards Rd, tel (01 232) 658 621, fax (01 232) 480 240.

Three-star purpose-built hotel, 4 miles out from centre, with serious orientation towards business guests. 8 meeting rooms accommodate up to 400. 106 bedrooms. Fax/photocopy/secretarial services. *See* also Best Places to Stay p 17.

WELLINGTON PARK HOTEL
21 Malone Rd, tel (01 232) 381 111,
fax (01 232) 665 410. Long-established, popular three-star hotel in the university area. 6 meeting rooms accommodate up to 180. 50 bedrooms. Fax/photocopy services. *See* also Best Places to Stay p 17.

BUSINESS INFORMATION

BUSINESS LIBRARY
Belfast Public Libraries, Royal Ave,
tel (01 232) 243 33, fax (01 232) 332 819.
UK and international trade directories; company information via Extel cards, McCarthy cards and press cuttings; market information in UK and international reports and statistics; CD-ROM and on-line database searching facilities; business newspapers and journals; UK and European patents information; fax and photocopying service.

LANGUAGE AND TRANSLATION

EXLINGUA INTERNATIONAL, 92 Lisburn Rd,
tel (01 232) 683 366, fax (01 232) 683 355.
An excellent reputation for a full range of services, from written translation, interpreting and video voice-overs to language training.

SECRETARIAL SERVICES

BELFAST BUSINESS TRAINING
Wilson's Court, 24 Ann St,
tel (01 232) 333 345, fax (01 232) 333 144, is a convenient city-centre agency offering typing, photocopying and fax services.

AUDIO-VISUAL EQUIPMENT

NIAVAC
34 Knockbreda Rd, tel (01 232) 645 391,
fax (01 232) 491 285. Wide range of equipment,
from large stage sets to single overhead
projectors.

EXHIBITION SERVICES

DIMENSION EXHIBITION INTERNATIONAL
Blaris Industrial Estate, Altona Rd, Lisburn
BT27 5QB, tel (01 846) 673 371, fax (01 846)
662 999. Stand contractors and designers who
can supply all exhibition needs, from hire of
portable stands, graphics and photography to
audio-visual equipment.

COMPUTER AND OFFICE SUPPLIES

MODERN OFFICE SUPPLIES
5 Donegall St, tel (01 232) 230 230. Long
established firm: five floors crammed with
business and office equipment of all sorts, from
quill pens to computer disks.

COURIERS

GROUP 4 COURIER SERVICE
tel (01 232) 771 770, fax (01 232) 781 700.
Highly rated for reliability. Bike service within
Belfast, same day delivery within N. Ireland or to
Dublin; overnight service to rest of Ireland and
UK; international service also.

LAUNDRY, DRY CLEANING AND IRONING

DUDS 'N' SUDS
37 Botanic Ave, tel (01 232) 243 956. American
franchise operation—an efficient laundromat with
complete range of laundering options including
express shirt service. Snack bar and large-
screen TV for those who decide on do-it-yourself

rather than drop-off approach. *Open Mon–Fri 8 am–9 pm, Sat 8 am–6 pm, Sun 12 noon–6 pm.*

LONG-STAY ACCOMMODATION

FLAT RENTALS
8 Lr Crescent, tel (01 232) 247 258, fax (01 232) 233 073. Reputable firm which provides furnished apartments for any period from one month upwards; kitchen equipment, crockery etc supplied; laundry and cleaning service on request.

SUGGESTED READING

- Jonathan Bardon *Belfast—An Illustrated History* (Blackstaff, 1982)

- J. C. Beckett et al *Belfast: The Making of a City* (Appletree Press, 1988)

- Peter Collins *The Making of Irish Linen* (Friar's Bush Press, 1994)

- Christopher Hill & Jill Jennings *Belfast* (Blackstaff Press, 1994)

- Robert Johnstone *Belfast: Portraits of a City* (Barrie & Jenkins, 1990)

- Sam McAughtry *Belfast Stories* (Blackstaff Press, 1993)

- W. A. Maguire *Belfast* (Ryburn, 1993)

- W. A. Maguire *Caught in Time — The Photographs of Alexander Hogg of Belfast* (Friar's Bush Press, 1986)

- Brian Walker *In Belfast Town—Early Photographs from the Lawrence Collection 1864–1880* (Friar's Bush Press, 1984)

CALENDAR OF EVENTS

The Northern Ireland Tourist Board publishes events guides several times every year. These are some of the highlights which recur annually in or near Belfast.

JANUARY
Holidayworld—International travel exhibition at the King's Hall, Belfast.

FEBRUARY
Belfast Musical Festival—Youth competitions in speech, drama and music; held every year since 1911, at the King's Hall, Belfast.

MARCH
Opera Northern Ireland Spring Season—at the Grand Opera House, Belfast.

APRIL
Tour of the North—International cycling race around Northern Ireland.
City of Belfast Spring Flower Festival—Major show mounted by daffodil societies and other floral associations.

MAY
Belfast Civic Festival—including the Lord Mayor's Show with floats and bands.
Belfast Marathon & Fun Runs—an epic race taking 4,500 runners all over the city.
Royal Ulster Agricultural Society Show—with international showjumping, sheepshearing, bands, at the King's Hall.

JUNE
Castleward Opera—Gala occasion in a delightful setting on the shores of Strangford Lough.
Proms '95—Ulster Orchestra symphony concerts at the Ulster Hall.
Maracycle—4,000 cyclists pedal between Belfast and Dublin.

JULY
City of Belfast International Rose Trials—Rose Week among the 100,000 blooms at Dixon Park, Belfast.
Battle of the Boyne Commemorations—Orangemen march on 12 July, anniversary of the

historic battle, in Belfast and 18 other towns.
Belfast-mid-Antrim Motor Run—Vintage day out for the Association of Old Vehicle Clubs.

AUGUST
Craigantlet National Hill Climb—Qualifying round of the RAC British National Hill Climb Championships.
Ancient Order of Hibernians Parades—Hibernians in green sashes march with banners and bands to mark Feast of the Assumption.
Ulster Grand Prix—International motorcycle racing at Dundrod outside Belfast.

SEPTEMBER
Opera Northern Ireland Autumn Season—at the Grand Opera House, Belfast.
Festival of Running—Bangor Classic 10K road race at Bangor, Co. Down.
Belfast Championship Dog Show—A Crufts qualifier all-breeds championship show at Balmoral, Belfast.

OCTOBER
Royal Ulster Agricultural Society Autumn Fair—Pigs and poultry show at the King's Hall, Belfast.
Ulster Antiques & Fine Art Fair—Well-established international collectors fair at Culloden Hotel near Hollywood, Co. Down.

NOVEMBER
Belfast Festival at Queen's—One of Europe's leading arts festivals, with excellent theatre, ballet, cinema and music of all kinds, in and around Queen's University, Belfast.

DECEMBER
Royal Ulster Agricultural Society Winter Fair—Dairy cattle show at the King's Hall, Belfast.
Horse Racing at Down Royal Racecourse, Maze.

USEFUL INFORMATION

CLIMATE AND CLOTHES

The longer your journey to Belfast, the more you may need to be reminded that the Irish obsession with weather stems from a cool climate more noted for rain than sun. Even in the summer, the weather can be colder and wetter than you might expect, so it's wise to pack woollens and a raincoat at any time of year. Looking on the bright side, the winters are rarely harsh, and spring or autumn can be every bit as pleasant as high summer. Visitors from other parts of Ireland are likely to find Belfast a degree or two colder than home.

HOW TO GET TO BELFAST

Access to Belfast is easy, by air, sea, rail and road.

AIR
You will fly into **Belfast International Airport**, Aldergrove, Co. Antrim, 19 miles west of the city centre, **tel 01 849 422 888**, or **Belfast City Airport**, 3 miles from town, t**el 457 745.** There is regular public transport from both airports into the city.

SEA
The fastest crossing from Britain to Belfast is the 90-minute trip from Stranraer on the **Seacat, tel 312 002.** You can also sail overnight from Liverpool on **Norse Irish Ferries, tel 779 090**; and in summer from the Isle of Man with the **Isle of Man Steam Packet Company tel 351 009**. There are sailings to Larne, 20 miles north of Belfast, from Stranraer with **Stena Sealink, tel (01 574) 273 616**, and from Cairnryan, **tel (01 574) 274 321**. Larne is linked to Belfast by bus and train services.

RAIL

Belfast Central Station on East Bridge St, about a mile from the centre, **tel 899 411**, is the main arrival point for travellers coming by train from other points in Northern Ireland, or from Dublin. For rail commuter travel within Belfast, Botanic Station is useful for the university area, and the new Great Victoria Street Station opening in October 1995 will in fact be Belfast's most central station.

ROAD

Ulsterbus, tel 333 000, operates buses to Belfast from all over Northern Ireland and, in conjunction with Bus Eireann, from Dublin. Depending on your point of origin you will arrive either in the Europa Bus Station, Glengall St, or Oxford Street Bus Station. Motorways—the M1, M2, M3 and the Westlink—make the city easily accessible by road.

HOW TO GET ABOUT IN BELFAST

BUS

Citybus, tel 246 485, operates throughout the Belfast area: a good bus map is available from tourist offices. Most buses depart from Donegall Sq in the centre, and bus stops are obvious on all major roads. Have small change ready to pay the driver as you board, or buy a multi-journey ticket in advance from newsagents or the Citybus Kiosk in Donegall Sq East.

TAXIS

These cost slightly less than in many other major cities. London-style metred cabs operate from airports and railway stations; private cabs are plentiful and can be booked by phone (consult the Yellow Pages), but not all have meters, so it is advisable to agree the fare in advance. The main city centre taxi rank is at Donegall Sq.

CAR HIRE

Hertz and Avis, the international giants, have bases at both airports and at Larne ferry terminal. **Belfast International Airport: Hertz tel (01 849) 422 533, Avis tel (01 849) 422 333. Belfast City Airport: Hertz tel 732 451, Avis tel**

452 017. Larne: **Hertz tel (01 547) 278 111, Avis tel (01 547) 260 799. Bairds, Boucher Rd, tel 247 770,** are among the better known local companies.

DRINK DRIVING LAWS
are strictly enforced: excess alcohol is defined as over 80 mg per 100 ml blood, 107 mg per 100 ml urine, 35 mcg per 100 ml breath.

SPEED LIMITS
70 mph on motorways, 60 mph on other open roads, 30 mph within built-up areas.

ROAD SIGNS
are in miles, not kilometres.

PARKING
In the city centre you should park either in an official car park (there are plenty, all very clearly indicated) or in a pay-and-display ticket zone on the street. The leaflet *Car Parking in Belfast,* available from tourist offices, has all the details.

NITB OFFICES

The Northern Ireland Tourist Board is extremely helpful and well worth contacting for information before or during your stay.

Belfast: St Anne's Court, 59 North St, Belfast BT1 1NB, tel (01232) 246 609, fax (01232) 240 960.

Dublin: 16 Nassau St, Dublin 2, tel (353 1) 679 1977, fax (353 1) 679 1863.

London: 11 Berkeley St, London W1X 5AD, tel (0171) 355 5040 or Freephone 0800 282 622, fax (0171) 409 0487.

Glasgow: 135 Buchanan St, Glasgow G1 2JA, tel (0141) 204 4454, fax (0141) 204 4033.

France: 3 rue de Pontoise, 78100 St Germain-en-Laye, France, tel (1) 39 21 93 80, fax (1) 39 21 93 90.

Germany: Taunusstrasse 52–60, 60329 Frankfurt, Germany, tel (069) 23 45 04, fax (069) 23 34 80.

USA: 551 Fifth Ave, Suite 701, New York NY 10176, USA, tel (212) 922 0101, fax (212) 922 0099.

Canada: 111 Avenue Rd, Suite 450, M5R 3J8, Ontario, Canada, tel (416) 925 6368, fax (416) 961 2175.

PRACTICALITIES

TELEPHONES
The code for Belfast is **01 232**. The international code for Northern Ireland is 44. In Belfast, some telephone kiosks take cash, some take phonecards obtainable from newsagents.

PASSPORTS, VISAS
You will need neither if you are coming to Belfast from any other part of Ireland or Britain. If you are arriving on a direct flight from further afield, the same rules apply as for visiting any other part of the United Kingdom.

CURRENCY
The pound sterling: 100p = £1.

VOLTAGE
240 V AC.

PUBLIC HOLIDAYS
New Year's Day; 17 March; Easter Monday; 1 May; 12 July; 25–26 December.

BANKING
Normal banking hours are Mon–Fri 9.30 am– 4.30 pm, with some city centre branches open until 5 pm on Thursday. Foreign currency can also be exchanged at Thomas Cook, 11 Donegall Pl, and at the post offices in Castle Pl, Donegall Sq and Shaftesbury Sq.

BANK HOLIDAYS
Banks are closed on public holidays (*see* above) and also on the last Monday in May and the last Monday in August.

POST OFFICES
Main locations Castle Pl, Donegall St and Shaftesbury Sq. Open Mon–Sat 9 am–5.30 pm.

CREDIT CARDS
Access/Mastercard and Visa/Barclaycard are the most commonly accepted credit cards.

EMERGENCY SERVICES
Dial 999 for fire, police or ambulance. For emergency medical treatment, British citizens require no special documentation; visitors from other EU countries will find it useful to have the E111 form with them; visitors from elsewhere are advised to arranged medical insurance for their trip.

TELEPHONE SERVICES
Operator: 100. Directory enquiries, Ireland or UK: 192. Directory enquiries, international: 153.

LICENSING HOURS
Mon–Sat 12 noon–11 pm,
Sun 12 noon–2.30 pm, 7–10 pm.

NEWSPAPERS
Belfast's three dailies are the evening paper, the *Belfast Telegraph*, which steers a middle course politically; the morning *Belfast Newsletter*, with loyalist leanings, and the more nationalist *Irish News*.

INDEX